Frontier Chapel to Spiritual Oasis

150 Years of Calvary Episcopal Church
ROCHESTER, MINNESOTA

To Joy,
For all the love and
joy you bring to Calvary
every week —
Love always,
Penny

Edited by:
The Venerable Canon Benjamin Ives Scott,
Barbara J. Toman & Penelope S. Duffy

Calvary 150th Celebration Book Committee:
Benjamin Ives Scott, Chair
Dulcie Berkman
Penny Duffy
Nancy Haworth Dingel
Dottie M. Hawthorne
Frank W. Hawthorne
Jan Larson
Barbara Toman

Cover photo by Penny Duffy, Rochester, MN
Cover and book design by Marjorie Durhman of Design Partners of Stiehm & Durhman,
Pine Island, MN
Printing by Davies Printing Company, Rochester, MN

Photo by Penny Duffy

Table of Contents

Foreword: A Spiritual Oasis for All 1

Chapter 1: The Episcopal Church in Frontier Minnesota. 9

Chapter 2: The Founding of Calvary Episcopal Church 17

Chapter 3: Calvary's Buildings and Fine Arts 29

Chapter 4: Chronology of Clergy. 51

Chapter 5: Children and Youth 67

Chapter 6: Faith Formation. 85

Chapter 7: The Altar Guild 91

Chapter 8: Music and Choral Arts 103

Chapter 9: Calvary's Churchwomen 117

Chapter 10: Social Action 127

Chapter 11: The Hospital Chaplaincy 141

Chapter 12: Fruitcake. 153

Chapter 13: Calvary and St. Luke's 165

Chapter 14: Slices of Life at Calvary 179

Index 195

Color Plates. 1-28

ACKNOWLEDGEMENTS

My thanks and praise to a gracious God whose Spirit has been present for 150 years in the people of Calvary Episcopal Church, Rochester, Minnesota, in the hearts and minds of those who have given generously and faithfully to produce this history of the parish, and in the sense of mission which will animate the ministry of Calvary Church for years to come. The story of this book, celebrating Calvary Church's 150 year history, has been the work of the sesquicentennial book committee and a team of writers. The Rev. Nicklas A. Mezacapa, the wardens, and the vestry have offered their prayers and encouragement and given us the funds to publish this history.

The committee made two decisions early on which give this book a distinctive character. It tells Calvary's story not in a chronology of clergy, but in selected topics which are told by individual writers. The committee also recognizes the value of the three previous histories of Calvary as rich archival resources. The committee invites the curious to examine the lists of names and dates in those well-done histories to find the people, places, and things that are prominent in them.

I have had the privilege of working with a committee and team of writers who have given their professional skills and experience, their time, and their goodwill with generosity. Their faithful dedication has made the production of this history a joy.

I worked with seven committee members. Barbara Toman and Penny Duffy edited the text of each chapter to give clarity and consistency to the entire book without losing the distinctive character of each chapter and writer. Their work has been invaluable. Nancy Dingel, Dottie and Frank Hawthorne, and Jan Larson served with me as both committee members and writers. Dulcie Berkman has rummaged in the dusty parish archives and the Olmsted County History Center for documents and photos. Bill Charboneau, Penny Duffy, and Cara Edwards were particularly generous in sharing their photos and taking additional photos at the committee's request. The committee received many scrapbooks, pictures, anecdotes, and tall tales from parishioners and organizations and is grateful for so much interest and so many resources. The book could include only a few of these offerings from the parish. The rest is now archival.

George Waters was involved in earlier histories and acted as adviser for the 150th book committee. He commissioned my task as chair to "birddog" the writers to complete the text and send it in on time. I had to "woof" only a few times. The generosity of Anne Allen, Dulcie Berkman, Nancy Dingel, Joe Gibilisco, Tim Hallett, Dottie and Frank Hawthorne, Marv Heins, Jan Larson, Nick Mezacapa, Barbara Toman, Brian Williams, and Penny Duffy, whose work is incorporated into the text, along with their cooperation and careful compiling of information, has provided the heart and core of this part of the 150th celebration at Calvary Church. To each of them, my thanks and praise.

------ Benjamin Ives Scott

The Oasis Courtyard

Photo by Penny Duffy

Foreword

A Spiritual Oasis in Downtown Rochester

Long before the Mayo brothers founded their famous clinic, a little brick church grew in Rochester, Minnesota. Calvary Episcopal is Rochester's oldest church building, having been established in 1860. The Mayo Clinic, which started in the 1890s, grew up around the church. For 150 years Calvary Episcopal Church has served as a worship center and spiritual outpost for Rochester residents and visitors. Having the Mayo Clinic as a neighbor has helped to focus and magnify our ongoing presence as a peaceful, healing oasis, dedicated to service in the spirit of Jesus Christ.

As a spiritual oasis, we offer the living waters of faith to those who call Rochester home, as well as to those who visit our city. Worship is the spiritual center of our parish life; as a congregation, we strive to balance our historic traditions with the ongoing gifts of the people and the needs of the community. Through faith formation we seek to teach God's ways and enable spiritual growth. As trusted servants, our mission is to be "doers of the word and not hearers only" (James 1:22a), carrying the transforming and healing power of God to all.

The architecture of our building reflects this commitment to spiritual healing and empowerment. Much of the structure dates back to the parish's founding and features the warmth of bricks, beams, and stained glass, offering a pleasant invitation to all. That invitation is enhanced by the flowers and park-like setting of the adjacent "Oasis Garden" and a parish program that has grown through time in scope and relevance.

All of these things are the products of a great congregation dedicated by faith to Christian service, wholesome stewardship, and the prayerful desire to deliver love and neighborhood into our 21st-century world. We welcome. We listen. We respond. We celebrate. We continue to be a dynamic outpost for the work of Jesus Christ!

Our Neighborhood

Calvary is one of a handful of places of worship in downtown Rochester. Our location in the midst of a world-class medical center helps define the healing presence that has become a vital aspect of our mission. Having visitors from all over the U.S. and various corners of the world, Calvary provides a spiritual connection and friendly assurance. It is not unusual for prayerful appeals to come from those far away, requesting that someone from the congregation make a pastoral visit to a person who is alone or in need of spiritual support. The members of Calvary and its clergy have always responded to these calls, gladly providing this long-distance spiritual connection. We are blessed by this friendly opportunity to serve.

Our church is open weekdays from 8 a.m. to 5 p.m. for prayer and meditation. Many people stop in during those hours to make intercession requests or offer thanksgivings on the listing provided in the narthex, and to choose from our ample supply of tracts and other literature that can be found there. The open, prayerful space invites the quiet presence of God. It is also quite common for Mayo Clinic patients to wander into Calvary for special events – a rummage or bake sale, or church forum -- and to strike up conversations with parishioners and to request prayers.

Nestled in the middle of the Mayo campus, we have the opportunity, given by God, to be engaged in the healing work that combines science and the Holy Spirit. This healing work is not, of course, confined to Clinic visitors. The members of our thriving parish family, many of whom are not connected to Mayo, are similarly involved in, and benefit from, Calvary's healing presence. We are blessed by the opportunity to serve from our unique corner of the world, and we work to live up to the responsibility given to us.

The Spiritual Oasis

Although Calvary has served Rochester and the world since the parish's founding, the specific notion of an "oasis" for all people began in 1986. At that time, Calvary's southeastern lawn was entirely enclosed by our memorial garden/columbarium and a thirty-year-old privet hedge. The hedge literally made it impossible for anyone within the church to see out, or anyone outside to see in.

The idea was to enhance this precious green space by removing the hedge and re-planting the area with flowers. Spurred by Dr. William Charboneau, a devoted member of the church who had a real passion for developing this vision, the new garden began to take shape. Sargent's Nursery and Ted Bartell, grounds manager for Mayo Clinic, were engaged to develop a plan that would transform what was a rather barren patch of lawn into a first-class "oasis garden." The plan included the present layout, multiple annual and perennial plantings (which the congregation would plant on a Sunday morning in May each year), a musical concert series, and park benches.

"The Oasis Garden" became a fixture for Rochester and its visitors, and solidified the metaphor for our ministry, launching a refreshed approach to our work and God-given presence. This peaceful space is provided deliberately, intentionally, and faithfully as an active space devoted to the healing grace of God.

Worship in the courtyard, summer 2000. The Rev. Nicklas A. Mezacapa distributes communion.

Photo by Bill Charboneau

During the summer months, Calvary hosts weekly lunchtime concerts in the Oasis Garden which have become hugely popular. The concerts feature local artists with music from around the world and instruments ranging from flutes to guitars to bagpipes. When Mayo's Gonda Building was under construction in 2000, workmen were spotted dancing atop the scaffolding to the rock 'n' roll music down in Calvary's courtyard.

The rest of the time, the garden remains a remarkable spiritual enclosure where flowers, trees, and cool grass provide a sharp contrast to the pace out in the street. When the weather is favorable, Clinic patients, employees, and others who work downtown come into the garden to eat lunch, re-group, or just find some quiet seclusion. When the weather turns cold, there, still visible, still available, in the midst of the plows, the salt and sand, the slush and rush of car and foot traffic, is a place where snow has fallen, "snow on snow," a hushed reminder of God's healing presence.

"We're Thinking Green Space"

Over the years the scope and reality of our oasis vision grew. By the early 1990s, the hotel located immediately north of Calvary had deteriorated, and was finally closed. Because of its proximity to the Clinic, there were murmurings about the property's future and potential value. The Clinic was interested, but Calvary was, too, and was preparing to make an offer of $250,000. "Visions of parking ramps danced in our heads."

Then, an outside firm stepped into the picture with a seven-figure offer for the property and a plan for a modern, international hotel. Two lawyers representing the new hotel came to the church from Los Angeles to present their scale model and make Calvary aware of the offer their clients had made, with what seemed to be an effort to leverage some kind of deal with the "bigger players." They presented their plan to the rector and wardens with professional finesse, concluding with the question: "Well – what are you thinking?" The rector and wardens looked at one another and replied, "We're thinking green space." The lawyers laughed. We didn't.

Meanwhile, Mayo Clinic and St. John the Evangelist Roman Catholic Church, northwest of Calvary, also expressed interest in the property. Coincidentally, the Clinic owned a piece of property adjacent to St. John's, and St. John's was willing to buy the hotel property for seven figures in a deal that would then allow them to trade it to Mayo for the Clinic-owned parcel they wanted. The plan simmered for a while, and then went through. St. John's bought the hotel property, traded it to Mayo for the land near their church, and Calvary would border a green space to be developed by the Clinic into the Feith Family Statuary Park.

"No Parking"

Parking in any downtown area is often at a premium. In Rochester, the compression that is generated by the Mayo campus and the healthy downtown economy seems to magnify the scarcity of parking even more! As part of Calvary's Oasis Building Project, launched in 2000, an inadequate driveway was replaced with a more practical drop-off driveway at the church's west entrance. Here, anyone who needs to stop by the church office during the week, when parking is most difficult, can do so without having to park several blocks away. Weekend parking requirements are accommodated by the multi-story ramp immediately north of the church, compliments of the Clinic.

Why bring up parking at all? Well, needless to say, Calvary is situated on a prime piece of real estate. We are right in the middle of an internationally renowned medical center, at the heart of a dynamic, growing city. Generations that follow may decide to consider whether a sprawling parking lot, which could make access much easier, would be a higher priority than remaining downtown. The decision, one would hope, would weigh convenience against vitality.

Calvary has always been, and continues to be, part of the very fabric of downtown Rochester. It is not just an historic building featuring quaint brick-and-beam architecture; it is the presence of Christ. We are a "Christian Station" with a unique healing and pastoral responsibility that in its time has offered peace and hope to thousands of people from all over the world, as well as to thousands of souls who call Rochester home. The need for this mission will never expire, and the Spirit of what Calvary can fire is a blessing to share for the ages of ages. May God's grace be served by our loving stewardship as we continue into this 21st century.

Nicklas A. Mezacapa

The Rev. Nicklas A. Mezacapa
June 7, 2009

Photo by Bill Charboneau

Minnesota in 1866

Map courtesy of Murray Hudson – Antiquarian Books & Maps, Halls, Tennessee.

Chapter 1

The Episcopal Church in Frontier Minnesota

By Anne Allen

The founding of Calvary Church in Rochester, Minnesota, was part of the Episcopal Church's effort to expand during the 19th century. Although its antecedents stretch back to the Apostles, the Episcopal Church itself is relatively new. It didn't exist in colonial America; Anglican churches in the colonies were outposts of the Church of England. At the end of the American Revolution in 1783, the parishes that had been part of the Church of England found themselves set adrift. Under the first amendment to the U.S. Constitution, promulgated in November 1791, they could no longer claim government support as the nation's established church. The earthly head of the Church of England is the British monarch; that arrangement was hardly possible in the new republic. There were no American bishops. Colonial parishes had been under the jurisdiction of the Bishop of London. In addition, Anglican priests were scarce in America, many of them having either returned to England or followed their Loyalist congregations to Canada.

An American Church

The American Episcopal Church's first challenge was thus to reorganize itself on a national basis. The consecrations of Samuel Seabury by the Episcopal Church of Scotland in 1784 and of William White and Samuel Provoost by the Archbishop of Canterbury in 1787 assured the American church of its proper place in the apostolic succession. The first General Convention, held in Philadelphia in 1789, laid the foundation of the church's organization and approved revisions in The Book of Common Prayer that would reflect the new church's American character. Rules were set up for the organization and recognition of dioceses and the training and ordination of clergy. Instead of a centralized administration under an archbishop, as in England, the church would be governed by a representative body, the General Convention, which would meet every three years to discuss matters of import to the church as a whole. Like the new U.S. Congress, this body would have two houses: a House of Bishops and a House of Deputies, the latter consisting of both lay and clergy. Each diocese would be responsible for organization and supervision of the parishes in its region.

As the church moved to organize dioceses in the original thirteen states, a massive population movement was taking place. Settlers from the original states and immigrants from Europe were crossing the Appalachian Mountains into the Ohio River valley and the southern shores of the Great Lakes where they began carving out new states in territory acquired from Native Americans through treaties. Many Protestant churches —Congregationalist, Methodist, Presbyterian, Baptist — allowed their faith communities to organize themselves, call a pastor, and then apply for affiliation with the national church.

The word "episcopal," however, means "based on the governing authority of bishops." Episcopal parishes exist only under the diocesan supervision of a bishop, making the process of starting parish churches more complicated. Eastern dioceses therefore sent missionaries west to organize parishes, and the General Convention established a procedure by which a group of parishes could come together, with episcopal permission, to organize a new diocese.

Mission work, conceived at the time as a way of carrying the Gospel to Native Americans and others unfamiliar with it, was initially carried out on an ad hoc basis. Volunteers were supported by individual parishes or by privately organized missionary societies, with the approval of the bishop in whose diocese these groups were located. In many of the new communities of the West, missionaries ministered not only to the un-churched but also to the faithful who wanted to worship as they had done previously in their homes back East.

The Rt. Rev. Jackson Kemper

Episcopal mission work in America and abroad was coordinated by the Domestic and Foreign Missionary Society, founded in 1820. Its Board of Missions gave stipends to missionaries to help with living expenses and the costs of establishing and running a mission. These stipends were very low, so most missionaries relied on additional donations from members of their missions and friends back home. If a diocese already had a mission program, the board often supplemented it. Board support was most effective in a new diocese's early years, when men and money to run missions were in short supply.

In 1835, the Rt. Rev. Jackson Kemper was consecrated as the Episcopal Church's first missionary bishop, appointed by General Convention to oversee the extension of the church into the new territories of Indiana, Missouri, and Michigan, which at that time included Minnesota. In the ensuing years most Episcopal missionaries in Minnesota were funded by the Board of Missions or another group, the Philadelphia Mission Society.

Inspired by Medieval Monastics

When Minnesota became a separate territory in 1848, the vast majority of its people were Native Americans of the Ojibwe and Dakota tribes. The only non-Native communities were Fort Snelling at the junction of the Minnesota and Mississippi rivers, a small trading settlement downstream at Pig's Eye (which would eventually become St. Paul), and a lumbering center at Stillwater. The Episcopal Church was represented by the Fort Snelling chaplain, the Rev. Ezekiel Gear.

In 1850, the Rev. James Lloyd Breck, founder of Nashotah House seminary in Wisconsin, came to St. Paul with two colleagues to set up a wilderness mission and school. Inspired by the medieval monastic missions which had spread the Gospel through Europe during the Middle Ages, Breck envisioned his mission as a center where missionaries could be trained and then sent forth to carry the Word of God to the "heathen," both "red and white." Although Breck hoped for a rustic site for his mission when he moved to St. Paul in 1850, the settlement there was soon on its way to becoming a city. In 1851, the U.S. government purchased some two million acres of potential farmland — nearly half of the future state of Minnesota — from the Dakota Nation. That purchase set off a land rush that raised the area's population to more than 150,000 within six years. Towns sprang up almost overnight throughout Minnesota Territory. The small chapel Breck had established in St. Paul rapidly evolved into the parish of Christ Church.

To serve the inhabitants of the growing territory, Bishop Kemper recruited missionaries from back East. He also suggested that Breck shift his focus from preaching to white settlers and establish a mission among the Ojibwe in northern Minnesota. In 1852, Breck set up a mission on Gull Lake near present-day Brainerd. Five years later, he expanded the mission, establishing a second site at Leech Lake, near present-day Bemidji. The federal government appointed Breck as official teacher for all the Mississippi Ojibwe.

Not all the Ojibwe approved of Breck's work. Hole-in-the-Day felt that the teacher should have been selected by the Ojibwe, not the government agent. Hole-in-the-Day and his followers attacked the missions in 1857, demanding that the government dismiss Breck and cease its tacit approval of his mission work. Breck moved most of his mission staff south to Faribault, about sixty miles northwest of Rochester. A small mission remained in operation at Gull Lake, led by the Native deacon John Johnson Enmegabowh, with support from a white missionary priest in Crow Wing.

At Faribault, Breck's Associate Mission regrouped. Although it held a school for Native children, called Andrews Hall, the mission's primary focus was serving white settlers and local Episcopalians. The Associate Mission founded Seabury Divinity School to train missionary priests and was instrumental in organizing parishes in the new towns along the rivers and railroads of southern Minnesota.

ENMEGABOWH

Originally a member of the Odawa tribe, Enmegabowh (One Who Stands Before His People) was born in Canada and converted to Christianity in his youth. He came to Minnesota in 1839 as interpreter for a Congregationalist mission. Brought into the Episcopal church by Rev. Gear, the chaplain at Fort Snelling, Enmegabowh was ordained a deacon by Bishop Kemper in 1859. In 1867, he became the first Native American ordained to the priesthood in the Episcopal Church. He served as missionary to the Ojibwe until his death in 1902. In 2000, his name was added to the Episcopal Church's national calendar; he is commemorated on June 12, the anniversary of his death. A copy of the icon of Enmegabowh, designed in 1997 by the Rev. Johnson D. Loud, Jr., hangs in Calvary's library.

Minnesota became a state in 1858. By the time the Diocese of Minnesota was organized in the same year, nineteen Episcopal clergymen were serving 52 parishes in the state, with several additional missions in various stages of organization. A few parishes were even able to support their own rectors.

The Rt. Rev. Henry Benjamin Whipple

Episcopal Services in "Every Village in the State"

In 1859, the General Convention endorsed the new Diocese of Minnesota and consecrated its first bishop, the Rt. Rev. Henry Benjamin Whipple. Whipple abhorred conflict among the faithful and worked throughout his tenure to keep factionalism from dividing the people of his diocese.

For example, during much of the 19th century, the Episcopal Church was wracked by an intense struggle between the High Church faction, which considered the church's central focus to be liturgy and one's participation in the communal life of a parish, and the Low Church faction, which was more concerned with the worshiper's individual salvation and connection with God. High Church Episcopalians favored candles and flowers on the altar, trained and vested choirs, weekly celebration of the Eucharist, formal celebrations of feast days, and other symbols of Christianity used by the Roman Catholic Church. Low Church or Evangelical Episcopalians celebrated the Eucharist only on special occasions, rejected all elaboration in weekly services as "Popish," and stressed preaching and individual Bible study.

Most Episcopalians fell between these two poles, in a vague area often called the Broad Church. However, passionate disputes were common. Breck's influence as a strong advocate of the High Church in the diocese of Minnesota's formative years was substantial, and there were occasional squabbles between his partisans and more evangelical missionaries. Although Bishop Whipple considered himself a High Churchman, his talent for calming the waters of dissension helped keep the Minnesota diocese free of the High Church-Low Church schisms that plagued many other dioceses.

Over the next forty years, Whipple became one of the best-loved clergymen in the state. He worked long hours raising money to support the diocese's mission work, established a diocesan mission board, and strengthened Seabury Divinity School at Faribault to provide priests for his diocese. He also founded two secondary schools, Shattuck School for boys and St. Mary's Hall for girls, under the auspices of the Associate Mission at Faribault. At his first diocesan convention in 1860, the bishop told the delegates that it was his goal to have Episcopal services held a minimum of once a month in "every village in the state."

Rochester was one of the first towns to benefit from Bishop Whipple's efforts.

Downtown Rochester, 1868. Calvary is the rectangular building in the right foreground. The extension to the original chapel is visible on the right.

Chapter 2

The Founding of Calvary Episcopal Church

By Anne Allen

George Head

In 1860, Rochester was little more than a hamlet of 1,180 souls on the prairies of southeastern Minnesota. But it was growing rapidly, as were many towns in the two-year-old state of Minnesota. The local newspaper, the *Rochester City Post*, observed that "Emigration still keeps pouring in upon us. On Monday last we noticed a large (wagon) train passing through our city accompanying which were eighteen head of horses, fifty or sixty head of cattle and about two hundred head of sheep." Five other churches were already organized in the town.

Rochester had been founded six years earlier by George Head, an English immigrant who grew up in Rochester, New York. In July 1854, he filed claim to the land where two roads crossed near the Zumbro River. One of the roads led west up the Zumbro from the Mississippi river town of Wabasha, the other came north from Dubuque, Iowa, to St. Paul. Head and his wife, Henrietta, built a log cabin at the crossroads; it became a popular stopping place known as Head's Tavern. The M.O. Walker Stage Line began service that same summer along the Dubuque Trail, and Head's Tavern became one of its major stops. Other claims were filed in the adjacent area, and in no time a little town had grown up. Head named the settlement Rochester because, he said, the sound of the falls on the Zumbro reminded him of his childhood home back in New York.

Rochester schoolchildren know the story of how George Head hitched his ox to a plow and dragged it through the brush due north from his cabin to make Broadway, Rochester's main street. What they probably don't know is that he was also one of the founders of Calvary Church. On Thursday evening, June 7, 1860, he was part of a small group of Episcopalians who gathered in a room beneath the second floor law offices of Charles C. Willson in the Union National Bank building, located on the corner of Broadway and Historic Third Street SW. They passed a resolution stating, "We believe that the interests of the church in this place would be promoted by the organization of a parish and that it be known and designated by the name of Calvary Parish." That same night, Head was elected to serve on the parish's first vestry, along with Willson, Herman C. Green, David Blakely, and William D. Hurlbut. John Arman Moore of Oronoco was the first senior warden, and J.F. Van Dooser was junior warden.

Photo courtesy of Olmsted County History Center.

The Union National Bank building, site of the meeting on June 7, 1860, at which local Episcopalians signed a resolution founding Calvary Church.

Accepting the Episcopal Society's Call

Episcopal services had been held periodically in Rochester since the summer of 1858, when the Rt. Rev. Jackson Kemper passed through town on his way to St. Paul. The great "Missionary Bishop of the Northwest," as he was called, was preparing to supervise the organization of a new diocese in Minnesota. In January 1859, the Rev. David Sanford, rector of the Church of the Good Shepherd in Faribault and a member of the Associate Mission headquartered there, held services in Morton Hall, located on the northwest corner of present-day Broadway and Second Street SW. A year later, on February 16, 1860, the new bishop of Minnesota, the Rt. Rev. Henry Benjamin Whipple, arrived in Rochester to meet with local churchmen and discuss the establishment of a mission to provide them with regular services.

After these meetings, on April 1, Bishop Whipple appointed the Rev. Charles Woodward, a representative of the Domestic Board of Missions who had come west to Minnesota, as Rochester's official missionary. "The Rev. Mr. Woodward of St. Paul has accepted the call of the Episcopal Society of this city," the *Rochester City Post* subsequently reported on April 7, "and will commence his labors about the first of May. Mr. Woodward, in addition to his duties as Rector, will open a select school for the higher English branches, German and French. A school of this character is very much needed in Rochester."

The proposed school never materialized. On May 9, however, the *City Post* announced that "Episcopal services were held at Morton Hall on Sunday under the direction of the Rev. Mr. Charles Woodward. Regular services will be held each Sabbath hereafter commencing at 10-12 o'clock in the morning and at 5:30 in the evening." By the end of that month, the Episcopal faith community was ready to organize itself into a parish. They pledged $265 to support their priest for the first year, only $186 of which was actually paid. The second year they pledged $150, which was

Charles Willson

The. Rev. Charles Woodward

paid in full. This was added to the annual $300 stipend that the Board of Missions paid its missionary.

From Founding to Building

It was Rev. Woodward who named the new parish "Calvary," after Calvary Church in New York City, where he had been ordained deacon in 1847. With the parish now established, the rector and vestry turned their attention to the challenge of building a church. In the meantime, Rev. Woodward continued to hold services in Morton Hall, in the First Ward School on College Street (now Fourth Street SW), and — on special occasions — in the courthouse, located on North Broadway on a site later occupied by the Avalon Hotel.

Fundraising also began. Like communities throughout the region west of the Alleghenies, new parishes in Minnesota often received substantial gifts from their fellow Christians on the East Coast. In March 1861, Bishop Whipple offered Calvary $500, matched by another $500 gift from a friend, the Rev. Morgan Dix, rector of Trinity Church on Wall Street in New York City. The gifts came with the understanding that the parish itself would raise an additional $500.

A committee consisting of Rev. Woodward and vestry members Willson and Blakely was appointed to secure and decide upon a location for the church edifice. Willson offered to donate some lots he had acquired on Main Street (now First Avenue SW), not far from the city hall. The offer was tentatively accepted by the vestry, and a building committee appointed. The vestry also voted to use red bricks from local kilns to build the church.

Apparently, some members of the parish objected to the proposed location, which was opposite the county jail. At its third meeting, on September 30, 1861, the vestry rescinded its previous action and instead directed the rector to "secure proper papers for lots 1, 2, 3 and 4, block 26, Original Plat, deeds to be made to Rt. Rev. H.B. Whipple, in trust for the Parish of Calvary Church, Rochester." These lots, on Zumbro Street (now Second Street SW), are where the present church stands. Lots 2 and 3 were donated by George Head, and the parish purchased the adjoining lots from Charles H. Lindsley, another member of the congregation.

With the land purchased, it was time to begin building. The building committee — consisting of the rector, parishioner Hiram T. Horton, and vestrymen Blakely and Hurlbut -- contracted with J.B. Alexander of Winona, who had built Episcopal churches in Stockton and Winona. By mid-1862, the necessary materials were beginning to accumulate: the bricks came from a kiln located near Eighth Street and Ninth Avenue SW; lumber was cut in nearby woods; glass for the windows arrived from the East, as well as benches to serve as pews. On May 6, 1863, the cornerstone was laid with great ceremony. In it, the rector placed a sealed metal box containing a Bible, The Book of Common Prayer, copies of church records, and one issue each of the *Rochester City Post* and the *Olmsted County Republican*. Afterward, he reportedly "made an excellent and appropriate address." The first service was held in the new church on July 12, 1863 —even though the glass windows were not yet installed.

The building of the little church, or "chapel," as it was described at the time, was achieved in the face of many difficulties associated with the Civil War, which began in April 1861 while the parish was still debating the location of its future home. In September 1862, as the building committee was gathering construction supplies, the First Minnesota

Volunteer Infantry regiment departed for Washington to serve with the Army of the Potomac. Raids conducted by the Dakota Nation on settlers in the region around the Minnesota River the previous month had sent waves of panic through frontier settlements throughout the state. A military-recruitment office opened in Rochester, and Dr. William Worrall Mayo, who had left his home in Le Sueur during the Dakota War to set up emergency hospitals to care for wounded settlers in New Ulm, was appointed examining physician of the enrollment board in April 1863. He moved his family to Rochester in 1864, and they became members of Calvary parish.

Dr. W.W. Mayo

Photo courtesy of Mayo Clinic Historical Unit

Through all this turmoil, Rev. Woodward labored steadily to raise the money and find the workmen needed to build his little chapel. Donations from parishioners appeared in the form of cash and labor. In 1863, the Calvary women's Sewing Society raised $115.65 for the building fund, and Loomis White, a friend of the rector, added $100 more.

By Christmas 1863, the chapel was complete. The *Rochester City Post* carried a full description of the Christmas program held that day. The red brick building measured 27 by 55 feet and was vaguely Gothic in style, a fashion then much in vogue among Episcopal parishes. The door, in the center of the building's south wall, opened directly onto the street. Its benches would seat approximately 100 people.

The rector's 1864 report to the diocese estimated the finished edifice to be worth $2,500. The lots were worth another $800 each, and the church's debt was only $70, "for materials." The parish had collected a further $1,025 toward the construction of a rectory, perhaps on one of the lots next to the church. By 1865, the church had 325 members, up from 223 in 1861.

The Abstract of Title reveals a series of threatened foreclosures on the land, beginning in 1861. The parish seems to have been able to find the necessary money to continue building, however, and in 1865, the title was officially transferred from Lindsley and Head to Bishop Whipple, as the representative of the diocese. The bishop held it until 1869, when he transferred it to the parish. Apparently, by that time he was convinced the parish was firmly established and capable of taking responsibility for its property.

A crowded calendar caused by the Dakota War and the Civil War as well as personal health issues prevented Bishop Whipple from coming to Rochester to consecrate the new church until January 28, 1866. Rev. Woodward's records at the end of that year show parish membership to be 350 souls, in 72 families. Eighty-two people were communicants, or baptized members in good standing who had been confirmed and were thus eligible to take communion. Among them were Louise (Mrs. William) Mayo, Charles and Annie Willson, Walter and Margaret Brackenridge, William Graham, and Samuel and Abbie Faitoute, all of whom would play a large role in the life of Calvary parish.

Photo courtesy of Mayo Clinic Historical Unit

Louise Mayo

Gifts from Well-wishers Back East

One of the first acts of the women's Sewing Society was to raise money to buy a portable melodeon, a small reed organ, for the rector to play to accompany the hymns. Rev. Woodward used it not only for services at Calvary, but also on missionary visits to nearby towns, carrying it with him alongside his communion set. In August 1864, the Sewing Society bought the church a Mason-Hamlin cabinet organ with a paneled black-walnut case. Purchased in Chicago, the organ was delivered on the newly built Winona and St. Peter Railroad, which passed through Rochester.

Well-wishers in the East sent gifts as well. In 1863, the parishioners of Christ Church in Shrewsbury, New Jersey, sent Calvary an Oxford Bible with Turkish binding for the lectern. The next year, B.B. Sherman of New York, who had provided the church with its first communion set (alms basin, urn, chalice and paten, all engraved "Calvary Church"), donated a 600-pound bell. Made at the Steel Bell Company's foundry in New York, it was Rochester's first church bell. Although little Calvary Church had no bell tower, the bell soon made its presence known. In April 1865, it celebrated the news of the fall of Richmond; a week later, it marked the death of President Lincoln. Its career was short, however. On January 29, 1870, the *City Post* sadly reported that Calvary's bell "is now 'dead broke,' and we shall never listen to its notes again."

In November 1866, Rev. Woodward resigned as rector of Calvary. Although he was only 45 years old, his health had been seriously damaged by the strenuous regime he had set himself, not only in Rochester but in the surrounding towns as well. He retired to a farm in Kalmar Township, seven miles west of Rochester, where he held weekly church services in a rural schoolhouse. In 1870, he left Minnesota for a teaching post at Andalusia College in Pennsylvania. He left behind a well-established parish filled with devout and energetic men and women well able to maintain the Episcopal Church's eminent place in the community.

ADDENDUM

Calvary's Founders

During the 19th century the Episcopal Church was frequently the religious home of a community's social and financial elite. Calvary conformed to this pattern. The Rochester citizens who worked with the Rev. Charles Woodward to form the new parish were men and women of standing in the community. Among the original vestry members:

- John Arman Moore, senior warden and treasurer, a wealthy farmer from near Oronoco.

- J. Franklin Van Dooser, junior warden, a hardware store owner. His wife, Sarah, was secretary-treasurer of the Sewing Society of Calvary Church (the rector's wife was president).

- George Head, Rochester's founder, a baker by trade. As Rochester grew, Head closed the inn he had operated from his log-cabin home, went into real estate and construction, and later opened a grocery store. Eventually, he sold the log cabin and built a new home on College (Fourth) Street SW, on the site now occupied by the Mayo Foundation House. Head's wife, Henrietta, hosted the first meeting of Calvary's Sewing Society at that house on June 14, 1860. She was active in the society until the family moved to Fergus Falls in 1873.

- Charles C. Willson, a lawyer whose office trained a number of men who later made names for themselves in the legal and political world. Among them were Mayo Foundation trustee Burt W. Eaton; U.S. Secretary of State and Nobel Peace Prize winner Frank Kellogg; and George Allen, a longtime Calvary vestryman and warden.

Willson's son, Bunn T. Willson, became a noted a judge and, like his father, served on Calvary's vestry. Charles Willson invested in Rochester real estate, acquired a 1,500-acre farm northeast of town, and built a mansion, Red Oaks, on Pill Hill at the intersection of Fourth Street and Ninth Avenue SW. His wife, Annie, often hosted church teas and youth events at Red Oaks. In 1892, Charles Willson served as official reporter for the Minnesota Supreme Court, editing and publishing the first twelve volumes of the court's decisions.

- William D. Hurlbut, Rochester's mayor in 1860. He speculated successfully in real estate, and he and his wife, Elizabeth, served on the committee that established the town's first library.

- David Blakely, owner of the *Rochester City Post*, the town's first newspaper. He served two terms as Minnesota's Secretary of State for Education. After leaving Rochester, he became manager of the *St. Paul Press* in 1874, and later ran the *Minneapolis Tribune*.

- Herman C. Green, a grocer. In 1870, he moved to South Dakota, where he founded the town of Mitchell.

On October 30, 1860, the parish held a second meeting in the Whitney Building to incorporate under the laws of the State of Minnesota. The certificate of incorporation was signed by Rev. Woodward as rector and witnessed by Charles Willson.

The other signatories were:
- John D. Ameigh, the parish clerk and a druggist who operated a combination book and drug store on College (Fourth) Street.

- John C. Cole, the owner of the Zumbro Flour Mill until he was killed by the 1883 tornado.

The other witnesses were:

- Dr. Cornelius S. Younglove, a physician with a large practice in Rochester.

- Moses W. Fay, a lawyer who had served as Rochester's first mayor, was judge of probate in 1863, and postmaster from 1866 to 1867.

Photo by Penny Duffy

Chapter 3

Calvary's Buildings and Fine Arts

By Benjamin Ives Scott

When Calvary's congregation moved into its new chapel in 1863, the parish had much to be thankful for. The threat of foreclosure on the property had been averted by a pair of timely $500 donations: one from the Rt. Rev. Henry Benjamin Whipple, the first bishop of Minnesota; and another from the Rev. Morgan Dix, the rector of Trinity Church on Wall Street in New York City. Combining those sums with $500 raised by the congregation, the parish was able to pay its bills. In spite of the scarcity of men and building materials due to the Civil War, the little brick church was ready for its first services.

On May 6, 1863, Calvary's first rector, the Rev. Charles Woodward, ceremoniously laid the cornerstone for the new church. It contained a metal box with a Bible, The Book of Common Prayer, and copies of the two local newspapers, *The Rochester City Post* and *The Olmsted County Republican*. The exact location of the cornerstone, however, has never been revealed. Two months later, on July 12, 1863, the congregation was worshiping in its new building. It is perhaps fortunate that it was summer, as the glass had not yet been installed in the windows.

The windows were the first of many additions and renovations to the buildings and grounds over the next 150 years. Throughout the ages faithful people have sought to glorify God by creating edifices and works of lasting beauty. Calvary's buildings and art are a testament to that aspiration. While the church has adapted to the practical needs of the parish and wider community, the central core of Calvary's mission remains evident in every change that has taken place. Like the Church itself, Calvary's building is constantly growing while maintaining its traditional warmth, grace, and stability. The congregation has been blessed with craftsmen, artists, and architects who, along with the generosity and commitment of parishioners, have contributed to enhancing the beauty and peace of the little brick church dedicated to the Glory of God.

Photo courtesy of Olmsted County History Center

Calvary Church, 1889. There were three rows of benches, with no center aisle.

From Chapel to Church

In 1863, Calvary Chapel, as it was then known, had the same overall appearance as the current church building, but the details were very different. The original building measured just 27 feet wide by 55 feet long, about one-third the size of the current building. It had a door opening directly onto Second Street SW, and was Gothic in style. The red bricks were locally made; Rev. Woodward and parishioner William Graham helped draw the bricks from the kiln at a yard near Ninth Avenue and Eighth Street SW.

Inside, the chapel apparently had partitions near the door across the nave, a common arrangement in small, rural churches. The space on either side of the door was used for coats, boots, tools, and stove wood. A cabinet contained worship appointments. There was no sacristy, undercroft, or storage area. There were few or no liturgical appointments, and the building was unheated except when in use. The floor was on one level. Benches to seat 100 filled the church in three rows beyond the partition, with a few chairs and a communion table that probably held a carved wooden cross in front. A rail may have separated the front area from the benches.

Photo courtesy of Olmsted County History Center

The south face of Calvary Church, 1894. The new entrance and window facing Second Street are visible.

Although services were held regularly in the new chapel starting at Christmas 1863, it was another six years before the bishop was confident enough in the parish's stability to turn over the deed for the lots to the wardens and vestry. On July 12, 1869, he and his wife, Cornelia, released the lots to the wardens and vestry of Calvary Church.

By that time, the rapidly expanding congregation had already outgrown its little chapel. Calvary's second rector, the Rev. William J. Johnstone, proved to be a popular speaker who, upon his arrival in January 1867, frequently filled the space with worshipers. The congregation decided to extend the building and make it less austere. In June 1868, the nave was extended north by 22-1/2 feet, and a cellar for a wood furnace was dug beneath. Continuing north, a 16-by-18-foot chancel was added, making room for liturgical services. To the east a 10-by-12-foot robing room was built, with an exterior entrance to the north.

Calvary Church at Christmas, 1895

Photo courtesy of Olmsted County History Center

Three rows of benches were also added for seating. The original clear glass windows were replaced with leaded stained-glass, a circular window was placed above the south entrance, and a new window was installed above the communion table. A walnut bishop's chair and a bench for clergy were added to the new chancel. Calvary already had a 600-pound bell, which had been donated in 1864; a tower where the bell could be hung was proposed, but not built.

Episcopalians now referred to the building not as a chapel, but as Calvary Church. To fund the building improvements and the parish's operating expenses, the vestry initiated pew rentals. They were announced each year on Easter Monday. In 1868, the vestry offered 30 pews for $40 per year, with nine free pews. It was not until 1894 that all pews became free.

Ironically, during the construction in 1868, Rev. Johnstone resigned, and for months, the enlarged building had services only occasionally for lack of clergy to conduct them. Indeed, during the next twenty years, Calvary had a succession of brief tenures by rectors. Often for months at a time, the parish had no rector and was served by students and faculty from Seabury Divinity School in Faribault. Throughout this period, however, the little brick church was carefully maintained and enhanced by the wardens and vestry. Some of these improvements facilitated worship; others provided more heat and light for the congregation's comfort.

The stone baptismal font, which is still in use, was placed in the front of the nave in 1871, a gift from the Sunday School. The following year, a cellar was dug under the front part of the church to install a second wood furnace, and oil-burning chandeliers were hung in the nave. In 1873, a Seabury Divinity student painted Bible verses on the walls between the windows. They were painted over in 1875 when the length of the church was carpeted by the churchwomen.

Calvary Church interior, 1897. Pews and a center aisle have replaced the original benches.

Calvary is particularly blessed in the beautiful woodwork that fills the church. In October 1880, Herman Kruschke, a local cabinetmaker, completed work on a walnut altar and reredos. The base of the present altar is Mr. Kruschke's work; his reredos now hangs on the wall near the northwest entrance of the church. In 1879, another local cabinetmaker, Thomas McCutcheon, built a walnut pulpit, which was added to the west wall of the nave. It was replaced in 1933 by an oak pulpit that was placed against the east wall of the nave. The 1879 walnut pulpit found a new home in Trinity Church, St. Charles.

Standing amid Devastation

The tornado of August 21, 1883, left Calvary standing amidst the devastation of the frame buildings surrounding it. That tornado was to change Rochester forever, as well as the mission and ministry of the little brick church. Dr. W.W. Mayo and his two sons, Dr. Will and Dr. Charlie

Photo courtesy of Olmsted County History Center

Calvary Church, viewed from the south, 1900. The Guild Hall, built in 1891, is visible in the background.

(all members of the parish), cared for the dying and injured in the local Buck Hotel, lodge rooms, and the dance hall. Mother Alfred of the Congregation of Our Lady of Lourdes proposed to the senior Dr. Mayo a hospital which the Sisters of St. Francis would own and he would run. On September 30, 1889, St. Marys Hospital opened on Second Street on nine acres of land just west of town. The doctors Mayo's offices were downtown on Second Street and First Avenue SW. Calvary Episcopal Church was located right in between.

As Rochester rebuilt, Calvary upgraded its little building. The improvements highlight technical innovations of the era as well as the congregation's growth. New oil chandeliers were installed in 1884; they were used for just five years before being replaced by gas fixtures in 1889. A white frame rectory was built on the property in 1885. With the parish once again outgrowing its building, the first Guild Hall was built in 1891 as meeting space for the Sunday School and the Parish Aid Society. Located north of the church, where Brackenridge Hall now sits, the Guild Hall was a one-room building measuring 27 by 32 feet, made of brick from the Winona kiln, with a door on the south side. Three years later, the original church entrance on Second Street SW was closed, and a stained-glass window installed in that opening. A vestibule entrance with frosted-glass windows was built on the southeast corner of the nave. Although this new entrance opened onto Second Street, the vestibule structure protected those in the nave from noise and cold. The plank sidewalks outside were paved with cement. Talk of building a bell tower continued.

Inside, the partition in the nave was removed, providing space for more seating. Two rows of oak pews replaced the original benches, leaving a center aisle. The walls were re-plastered and painted with stenciling above the wainscoting. The sanctuary furniture was now all of walnut, and the altar rail of iron with scrollwork. In 1900, a 20-by-30-foot annex was added to the Guild Hall to the north, with a 10-by-20-foot kitchen attached.

At the start of the 20th century, Calvary entered a period of strong growth and prosperity. The church's interior was redecorated once again, its structure beginning to look more as it does today. The entire chancel floor was raised three steps to the choir and three more steps to the altar. Two ornamental arches were added to the chancel, and six decorative trusses with a birch paneled ceiling installed above the nave. The carved wooden cross was moved from the altar to the west chancel niche, and a duplicate was carved for the east niche to provide balance. The gas fixtures were replaced with electric lighting. The pulpit was moved from the chancel to the main floor. In 1904, a W.W. Kimball lever-pump pipe organ replaced the cabinet pump organ. The console was on the east side of the chancel, the organist facing north.

Meanwhile, Calvary's founding generation was passing away. Their children sought to memorialize them, particularly with generous

Harold Crawford

donations of stained-glass windows that have become some of the best-loved features of Calvary Church. In 1904, the window above the altar — made in the Tiffany studio and depicting "Christ Blessing the Children" — was installed. It was the gift of Edith Graham Mayo and Dr. Christopher (Kit) Graham, in memory of their mother, Jane T. Graham, and in honor of their father, Joseph Graham. A year later, two smaller windows were placed on either side of the reredos, a "Head of Christ" and "Ecce Homo" made by Pittsburgh Glass. In the nave and choir, stained-glass windows, installed between 1904 and 1907, replaced the 1865 leaded stained-glass windows. The vestry sold the old leaded windows in 1917.

The Rev. Arthur H. Wurtele accepted the position of rector in 1912 and would soon be married. To provide a home for the couple, the vestry moved the old white frame rectory to the north of the church, tore down an adjacent barn and built a new brick Tudor-style rectory with an entrance facing Third Avenue SW. The old rectory was renovated in 1923 for use by the Girls' Friendly Society. In subsequent decades it housed the sexton's family and became known in the parish as the Seaman house. It was demolished in 1962.

Harold Crawford: the "Pill Hill" and Calvary Architect

In its formative years, the fashionable street in Rochester was Second Street SW, running west from Broadway. Traffic moved across the city between downtown businesses, hotels, and the Mayo Clinic to St. Marys Hospital on the west edge of town. When Dr. Will Mayo chose a location up the hill to build his home, now the Mayo Foundation House, the surrounding area became a popular residential area for Mayo's physicians. The shaded, sloping streets soon had a number of stately homes and

became known as "Pill Hill." Many
of the Pill Hill homes and other
buildings in town were designed
by Harold Crawford, a Calvary
parishioner.

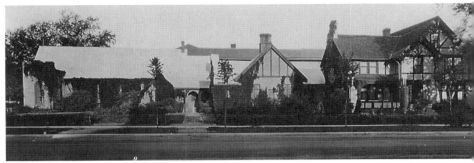

Calvary Church, east side, 1925. The Tudor rectory, built in 1912 and demolished in 1967, is on the right.

For the next seventy years
Calvary was fortunate to have Mr.
Crawford as an "in-house" architect
and artist. Through the generosity of
Blanche Graham, wife of Dr. Graham,
the vestry engaged the young architect to design a new parish hall. In
1917, the old brick Guild Hall was replaced with Brackenridge Hall,
named for Mrs. Graham's mother, Margaret Brackenridge.

Mr. Crawford's work can be seen in almost every part of Calvary's
building. Inside the church, he enlarged the altar; outside, he moved
the entrance to the vestibule from the south to the east. The bell tower
was not forgotten. Mr. Crawford was asked to proceed with plans for
its construction above the vestibule; however,
due to cost considerations in 1917, those plans
were set aside. One technical innovation that the
congregation surely welcomed at this time was
the installation of an electric blower for the pipe
organ, which meant volunteers no longer had to
work the lever-pump by hand.

By this time, Calvary Church looked like a
small campus, consisting of several unconnected
buildings: the church itself; Brackenridge Hall;

The new lych-gate entrance, 1950.

Photo courtesy of Olmsted County History Center

Calvary Church, 1948. The W.W. Kimball pipe organ, installed in 1933, is on the left. Windows flank the altar.

the "old rectory," also known as the Seaman house; and the Tudor rectory. The latter was needed in 1933 to house the diocesan hospital chaplain, who ministered to patients at the Mayo hospitals. The vestry bought a house "off campus," at 1150 First St. SW, for the then-rector, the Rev. Guy C. Menefee, and his family.

The discussion about building a bell tower atop the vestibule continued for decades. Eventually, however, Mr. Crawford proposed a covered walkway extending from the vestibule's east-facing entrance. The vestry approved the construction of this lych-gate in 1950 as a memorial to Rev. Wurtele. The two small windows on either side of the altar were moved to the north wall of the vestibule.

The Post-War Space Debate

By the time the Rev. O. Wendell McGinnis accepted the position of rector in 1954, Calvary was caught up in the post-war baby boom. Rev. McGinnis came to Rochester anticipating changes to the little brick church to accommodate the needs of a congregation that, once again, had outgrown its structure. In addition, city planners had their eye on the church site. As early as 1931, the site had been considered for a new post office.

The Mayo Foundation also was interested. In 1958, it presented to the vestry a plan for buying Calvary. With the encouragement of Bishop Kellogg and a ground-swell of the congregation, the vestry voted on June 17, 1958, to retain the downtown site across from Mayo Clinic and build a parochial mission in suburban Rochester. Eventually, the Mission would become the independent parish of St. Luke's. This decision would have far-reaching implications for the mission and ministry of Calvary, soon to be the oldest church building in Rochester.

Photo courtesy of Olmsted County History Center

Calvary Church, 1950, after the altar windows were removed.

At its 100th anniversary the parish was reported to have 1,400 baptized members and construction was underway at two sites. The cornerstone of the mission was laid on a 4 ½ acre site northwest of downtown Rochester on October 30, 1960. At the downtown site a new sacristy was annexed to the west wall of the chancel with an adjoining restroom, staircase, and exterior entrance. The kitchen was redesigned, and the basement of Brackenridge Hall was restructured with renovated meeting rooms, a new furnace, and electrical service. On the east side, the porch connecting the old sacristy with Brackenridge Hall was enclosed, and the narrow passage between the buildings opened to the organ chamber. The buildings which housed the little brick church were now connected to one another. On the north side of the property there remained the old white-frame sexton's house and the Tudor-style residence for the hospital chaplain.

Photo courtesy of Olmsted County History Center

Calvary Church, east side, 1969. The new office and Christian Education wing are visible, as well as a young hedge surrounding the courtyard.

When the Rev. Samuel Cook accepted the position of rector in 1965, he sought to move the congregation from a conflicted survival-and-reorganization mentality to a renewed focus on outreach and community service. The nave was redecorated in blue, and wheelchair ramps installed. In 1966, through the generosity of Dr. and Mrs. Charles W. "Chuck" Mayo and Mrs. Frances Gooding, a 200-year-old bell was brought from a little town no longer on the map, Tamarack, Wisconsin, and hung in a small arch above Brackenridge Hall. Thus ended the century-long, unsuccessful effort to install a bell tower!

That same year, the little brick church was designated an Historic Site by the Olmsted County Historical Society. A bronze plaque was placed at the original entrance on Second Street. The following year, a carved reredos was placed above the altar beneath the Tiffany window, with panels designed by Harold Crawford placed on either side. Carved with the Eucharistic symbols of wheat and grapes, the panels were later moved to the columns in the chancel.

The vestry addressed the urgent need for Sunday School and meeting room space by voting to build an educational facility. To make room, the Tudor residence — where the hospital chaplain had lived until 1952, and where the church offices had been located since -- was demolished. In 1968, construction began on a new building with classrooms, offices, meeting rooms, and an apartment for the church sexton. The new entrance on Third Avenue SW honored the memory of Rev. McGinnis. That same year, the 1894 window installed in the opening of the original entrance on Second Street was removed and stored, and replaced with a new window depicting the Sermon on the Mount.

Photo courtesy of Olmsted County History Center

Calvary Church, 1986. The Crawford reredos was installed in 1967.

In addition to building extra space, the parish worked to improve its existing worship area, allowing Calvary to incorporate changes then underway in Episcopal liturgy. In 1974, the current Noehren-Harris pipe organ was installed, along with improvements to the sound and lighting systems. In 1978, the vestry approved the construction of an enclosed ambulatory to facilitate moving people from the lych-gate entrance to Brackenridge Hall. No longer did parishioners — not to mention brides walking to the back of the church — need to venture outside. The new passageway lighted the existing nave windows artificially. The small windows on the old vestibule's north wall were moved to the ambulatory's exterior wall and flanked by two new adjoining windows. The Gothic window from the old Second Street entrance was removed from storage and placed in the old sacristy.

Amid much concern about maintaining the church's exterior appearance, the parish was able to acquire bricks from a building being demolished in Winona. The bricks had been made in the same Winona kiln from which Calvary had obtained materials for an earlier

Photo by Penny Duffy

Calvary Church columbarium

construction. During the 1978 renovation Calvary's sanctuary altar, which, like most Episcopal altars at the time, stood against the wall, was moved three feet forward, giving room for the celebrant to face the people. The ambulatory was completed in 1982, and the parish dedicated it to the memory of Rev. Cook in 2008.

The Columbarium

Rev. Cook considered a columbarium to be a valuable dimension to Calvary's ministry. After exploring several alternatives, the vestry concluded that locating the columbarium in the churchyard, where the interment of cremated remains could be left directly in the ground, was best. A brick wall was constructed on the southeast corner in memory of Frederick William Schuster. The names of the interred are engraved on plaques on the courtyard side of the wall. On the street side is a Celtic cross designed by Harold Crawford. That cross, known in the parish as "the Crawford cross," is also used on the nameplate of the parish newsletter as well as on the western wall of the church. The columbarium was dedicated on September 23, 1984, with the interment of the ashes of Frank Watson and the Rev. James Peck.

An Oasis amid Skyscrapers

Over the years the Mayo Foundation had acquired all of the buildings immediately surrounding Calvary and constructed a towering medical center campus downtown. In 2008, Rochester's Mayo Medical Center employed 32,348 people, saw over 1.5 million out-patients, and admitted 61,664 patients to its hospitals. The mission of Calvary Church in downtown Rochester and its ministry among its members became increasingly focused and clarified as a spiritual oasis serving the parish and the community.

Recent improvements and renovations have tried to meet those needs. In 1998, the Mayo Foundation bought the only other building on Calvary's block, the former Virginia Hotel. It and an adjacent parking garage were demolished to make room for the Feith Family Statuary Park. Prominent in the park and facing Calvary's north windows are two larger than life statues depicting Mother Alfred and Dr. William Worrall Mayo, discussing the founding of St. Marys Hospital. Two other statues depict the Mayo brothers, Dr. Will and Dr. Charlie. Between the park and Calvary's north wall, a new street curves round to the Mayo Clinic's main entrance at the Gonda Building.

The Rochester Post-Bulletin, Dec. 30, 2000

Suddenly, the old alley entrance to Calvary had become a conspicuous façade, visible from the main entrance of the Mayo Clinic. Once again, the congregation faced decisions. Should it address deferred maintenance and/or expand? How could the 19th-century structure meet modern building-code requirements?

Photo by Penny Duffy

Calvary Church education wing, viewed from the north in 2009 with the third floor addition visible. The renovated north side faces the Mayo Clinic's Feith Family Statuary Park and the street leading to the main entrance of the Mayo Medical Center.

In his vision for the parish's mission in the middle of the Mayo Clinic, the rector, the Rev. Nicklas A. Mezacapa, coined the phrase "Spiritual Oasis." On October 14, 2001, at a special parish meeting, the congregation unanimously approved the Spiritual Oasis Project with an initial funding of $1.7 million to renovate the north side of the building. It was to include a new floor above the Christian Education wing, with meeting space that could be a resource for the parish and wider community; remodeling of existing meeting rooms and of the classroom and music areas; construction of a new nursery; and installation of an elevator, an improved wheelchair ramp, and handicapped-accessible restrooms.

The vestry was adamant that the main, historic portion of the church not be altered and that the new construction should blend in architecturally with the old. Retaining the brick façade, the addition unified the complex and made it compatible with its urban environment. Landscaping on the property line joining Mayo's statuary park created a green area in the medical complex. The large meeting room on the new third floor was named "Crawford Hall" in memory of the architect who so shaped Calvary. Watercolor pictures painted by Mr. Crawford, depicting still lifes and Rochester buildings that had been torn down over the years, were hung on the walls. The two other upstairs rooms were named to honor the Mezacapa and Roenigk families. At the project's groundbreaking in 2002, a time capsule was sealed in the cornerstone to be removed and opened in 2102.

The little brick church had grown into a spiritual oasis in the midst of a world-renowned medical center. Calvary celebrates its 150th anniversary greatly blessed by the generosity of those named and un-named parishioners who have supported the church's ministry through the years. Its buildings and grounds offer a home for that work and a sacred space within the ever-changing community.

A D D E N D A

The Needlepoint

Calvary's beautiful kneelers are covered in needlepoint made by parishioners working with the National Cathedral's Ecclesiastical Needlepoint guidelines. At the request of Rev. Cook, parishioner Bette Dines led the initial effort to complete fifteen kneelers, which were dedicated in 1979. Designed with the theme of the church seasons, the kneelers have appropriate symbols and the initials of the person who did the work, all in a red background.

Additional needlepoint cushions were designed at the suggestion of Rev. Mezacapa. The most recent cushion covers a bench in the north entrance. It was designed by Bette Dines in memory of Sarah Dines, and includes ecumenical symbols and the commission to go forth into the world to help the afflicted and to honor all people. The doorway, which lies adjacent to Mayo Clinic, articulates the inclusive and healing mission of Calvary Church.

Watercolors

Calvary Church has two collections of watercolors which are framed and hung in its public meeting rooms.

In 1975, Harold Crawford gave to the parish a collection of watercolors he had painted of historic Rochester buildings, floral arrangements, and American church buildings of historic and architectural significance. Many of the Rochester buildings depicted are now lost to development. Most of the Crawford watercolors hang in Crawford Hall; others may be found in the Fireside Room and the library.

In Menefee Hall and the parish office hang a collection of watercolors by parishioner David Dines. A gift of the Dines family in 2007, they depict a gentle, rural Minnesota landscape.

The Windows

Above the altar

Christ Blessing Little Children, Tiffany Studio, New York, in memory of Jane T. Graham and in honor of Joseph Graham; gift of their children Edith Graham Mayo and Christopher Graham, 1904. (plate 1)

Choir, west wall

Saint Cecilia, in memory of Mrs. Emma F. Judd; gift of Edward J. Judd and Cornelius M. Judd, 1905.

Nave, west wall, north to south

Cross and Crown, in memory of Q. B. and S. Blakely; gift of Amerst and Amelia Blakely, 1905.

Resurrection, in memory of William Brown; gift of Adelaide Brown, 1905.

Palm Sunday, in memory of Musetta, John, and Richard Graham; gift of Edith Graham Mayo and Christopher Graham, 1905.

Chalice with Grapes and Ivy, Tiffany Studio, New York, in memory of John Graham and Jennie Graham Williams; gift of Edith Graham Mayo and Christopher Graham, 1905. (plate 2)

Lilies of the Field, Tiffany Studio, New York, in memory of the Brackenridge Family; gift of Margaret Brackenridge and Blanche Brackenridge Graham, 1907. (plate 3)

Nave, east wall, north to south

Lamp of Knowledge, in memory of William and Ann Bird; gift of Mrs. George Washington Waldron, 1905.

The Greek Cross, in memory of Henry Curtis Butler; gift of Martha Butler, 1905.

Cross and Crown in a Landscape, in memory of Samuel Day Faitoute and Abbie Frances W. Faitoute; gift of Carrie Haines and Frances Gooding, 1907.

Small Cross, Tiffany Studio, New York, in memory of the Brackenridge Family; gift of Margaret Brackenridge and Blanche Brackenridge Graham, 1907. (plate 4)

Ambulatory, north to south

- A Gothic window, 1894, originally installed in the opening of the south wall of the nave, the original entrance to the church; gift of Huber Bastian. The window remained in the nave until 1966, when it was replaced by The Sermon on the Mount. The Gothic window was moved to the ambulatory when the passageway was completed.

- *The Blessed Virgin Mary*, Rochester Stained Glass Window Co., in memory of Jennie Alice Scott; gift of Benjamin and Sarah Scott, 1982, after a watercolor by Harold Crawford of a window at Chartres Cathedral, France.

- *Head of Christ*, Pittsburgh Glass Co., in memory of the Rev. Charles Woodward; gift of Margaret Brackenridge, 1905.

- *Ecce Homo*, Pittsburgh Glass Co., in memory of Bishops Henry Benjamin Whipple and Mahlon Norris Gilbert; gift of parishioners, 1905.

- Husband Family Window, Rochester Stained Glass Window Co.; gift of the Richard L. Husband family. The window depicts the Mayflower ship, Bishop H. B. Whipple, Bishop Samuel Seabury, Seabury Divinity School in Faribault, Minnesota, Seabury-Western Theological Seminary in Evanston, Illinois, and various symbols relating to the Husband family, 1982.

Vestibule, south wall

Native Americans Receiving the Gospel, in memory of the Rev. William Wallace Fowler; gift of his sons, 1950. (plate 5)

Nave, south wall

- Rose Window, placed above original entrance, 1868.

- *Sermon on the Mount*, in memory of Glen Meyers Waters; the gift of George F. Waters, 1968. (plate 6)

East entrance to educational building

Designed by Harold Crawford in 1969, the four lancet windows on the north wall were given in honor of the Rev. O. Wendell McGinnis and Fred Reed; and on the south wall, in honor of Arthur Sachs and Harry Wood. Crawford's watercolor of the windows hangs in the library. (plate 8)

North entrance to educational building

Completed in 2007, the window develops a healing theme from the Gospels, interweaving the heavenly and earthly dimensions to Jesus' ministry. Kjerland Stained Glass Studio, Northfield, Minnesota, designed and executed the window. (plate 7)

In the six healing panels on the west side, top to bottom:

Healing Jairus' Daughter, gift of Dean and Jan Larson

Restoring Sight to the Blind Man, gift of John and Beverly Spittel, Jr.

Healing the Centurion's Servant, gift of David and Bette Dines

On the east side, top to bottom:

The Paralytic Man, the gift of the Inwards family

Healing the Hemorrhaging Woman, the gift of Al and Sandra Hunter

Woman Loosed from Infirmity, the gift of Calvary Episcopal Churchwomen

Above the healing panels is a circular window depicting an angel in memory of Eleanor Judd Kirklin, the gift of her family. Framing the healing panels are three Gothic panels above and two below, sponsored by the wardens and vestry.

Photo by Penny Duffy

Chapter 4

Chronology of Clergy

By Benjamin Ives Scott

The story of the clergy who have served Calvary Church begins like the stories of many other clergy serving little frontier towns. In 1860, Rochester was a small and isolated farming community with an entrepreneurial and somewhat transient population. There were many such villages with promise along the major rivers and, later, along the major railroads. Some towns and their small Episcopal churches survived, and some did not. Calvary's chronology of clergy reflects these humble beginnings and the parish's growing sense of mission in what would become Minnesota's third largest city.

The Associate Mission community in Faribault was instrumental in initiating the organization of parishes in the new towns across southern Minnesota. In January 1859, the Rev. David Sanford came to Rochester to meet with the men who would establish Calvary Episcopal Church. Rev. Sanford gathered a congregation for services in Morton Hall and guided the congregation through the requirements of the newly constituted civil and canon laws regarding religious institutions. In February 1860, the Rochester Episcopalians were ready to meet with the new bishop of the Diocese of Minnesota, the Rt. Rev. Henry Benjamin Whipple, and receive the appointment of a priest to serve as rector of the parish.

Some past rectors of Calvary Church. Top row, from left: Charles Woodward, Jason F. Walker, William W. Fowler, Arthur H. Wurtele. Bottom row, from left: William W. Daup, Guy C. Menefee, O. Wendell McGinnis, Samuel W. Cook.

The Rev. Charles Woodward, April 1, 1860 to Nov. 1, 1866

On April 1, 1860, the Rev. Charles Woodward became Calvary's first rector. He was born in Somersetshire, England, on July 3, 1821. His family came to America in 1825, settling in Tompkins County, New York. Rev. Woodward graduated from Hobart College in 1844 and General Theological Seminary in 1847 and was ordained a deacon on June 27th of that year at Calvary Church in New York City. After taking a walking tour of Europe, he was ordained a priest at Trinity Church in Geneva, New York, in 1851.

He served at Seneca Falls, New York, and Middleton, New Jersey, before moving to St. Anthony Falls, Minnesota. There he served as the associate rector at Holy Trinity Church and tutored at the parish school for boys at Christ Church, St. Paul. He participated in the formative conventions of the Episcopal Church in Minnesota in 1857, 1858, and 1859, presided over by the Rt. Rev. Jackson Kemper, Missionary Bishop of the Northwest. The 1859 convention elected Henry Benjamin Whipple the Bishop of Minnesota.

Accepting the appointment of the new bishop and moving to Rochester in April 1860, Rev. Woodward led Calvary Church (which he named after Calvary Church in New York City) into union with the diocese in June 1860 and into incorporation with the state the following October. He negotiated securing the lots of the present church after other locations were explored, and laid the cornerstone of a little brick Calvary Chapel in 1863. In addition to holding services in Rochester, he conducted services in nearby High Forest, Pleasant Grove, Chatfield, Hamilton, and Oronoco, often traveling on foot. He also supported the missions in Austin and other new towns in Mower and Fillmore counties.

On November 1, 1866, he retired to a farm in Kalmar Township, Olmsted County, due to poor health. Four years later, he and his family moved to Philadelphia, where he taught languages at Andalusia College. He died at the age of 70 on November 7, 1891, leaving his wife and seven children. He and his wife, Charlotte, are buried at Oakwood Cemetery in Rochester.

The Rev. William J. Johnstone, Jan. 1, 1867 to June 1, 1868

With Charles Woodward's resignation in November 1866, the wardens and vestry looked again to Faribault. William J. Johnstone was among the first three to graduate with a Bachelor of Divinity degree from Seabury Divinity School. He accepted the position at Calvary Church on January 1, 1867. Parish records reported that he was popular and well-spoken. During his brief year-and-a-half tenure, he baptized 67 individuals and presented 60 for confirmation. He filled the little brick chapel, and work was begun on enlarging the building and adding a bell tower. He resigned, however, on June 1, 1868, to serve in the Diocese of Illinois.

The Rev. David P. Sanford, March 13, 1869 to July 10, 1870

When Rev. Johnstone resigned, the wardens and vestry once again turned to Faribault. After a nine-month search, the Rev. David Sanford accepted the position. Rev. Sanford had been the consultant from the Associate Mission in Faribault who had assisted in organizing what would be named Calvary Church. He had worked with Bishop Kemper in organizing congregations in the fledgling diocese, becoming the first rector of the Parish of the Good Shepherd in Faribault and a tutor in Seabury Divinity School. He had returned to his home in Wolcottville, Connecticut, when Calvary's vestry persuaded him to come back to Rochester. He accepted the position in March 1869, presiding in the newly enlarged building. Rev. Sanford held the position for a year and four months when he resigned and returned to Connecticut in poor health.

The Rev. Alpheus Spor, Aug. 5, 1870 to Jan. 30, 1872

With Rev. Sanford's resignation in July the wardens and vestry hastened to search for a new rector, inviting the Rev. Alpheus Spor, rector of St. John's, Mankato, to move to Rochester. Accepting the position, he purchased a home on the lot at the rear of Calvary and remained a little over a year. At his resignation in January 1872, he continued missionary work at Rushford, Caledonia, and Brownsville. He died in 1877 while en route to a diocesan council meeting in Faribault. Near Houston his horse was startled by a passing train. Rev. Spor was thrown from the buggy and run over by the buggy wheel. The baptismal font in the present Calvary Church was given in his memory from the Sunday School.

The Rev. Alexander W. Seabrease, May 1, 1872 to April 1, 1875

After Rev. Spor's resignation on January 30, 1872, the wardens and vestry searched through the winter, and called the Rev. Alexander Seabrease from Salisbury, Maryland. He purchased a house near the little brick church and continued the mission stations at Chatfield, Hamilton, High Forest, Pleasant Grove, Oronoco, and Mantorville. Under his pastoral care Calvary developed an active Sunday School. In the church building a stove was installed under the floor near the entrance so that, as was said at the time, "hereafter the congregation will have an opportunity to warm themselves … before taking their seats." During his time at Calvary, oil-burning chandeliers were hung over the center aisle, and an elegant carpet covered the floor. The interior of the church was painted, and a Seabury Divinity Student stenciled Bible verses in Old English letters between the windows. At his resignation Rev. Seabrease moved to the Diocese of Illinois.

The Rev. Jason F. Walker, June 1875 to Oct. 1, 1876

The wardens and vestry had met the Rev. Jason Walker upon his marriage to Martha Cowles at Calvary in December 1866. During the winter of

1875, he was guest preacher at Calvary and continued as a guest after Rev. Seabrease's resignation. He accepted the position as rector on June 1, 1875, agreeing to remain one year from September 1, 1875. Keeping to his agreement, he resigned October 1, 1876, and moved to the Diocese of Colorado. From October 1876 to September, 1877, Calvary was closed for lack of clergy, a situation not uncommon on the frontier.

The Rev. John Keble Karcher, Sept. 16, 1877 to October, 1878

In late 1877 the Rev. John Keble Karcher re-opened Calvary with regular Sunday services and prepared the congregation for a splendid Christmas celebration. "The interior of the church was beautifully decorated, festoons of evergreens hanging from the ceiling to the windows and wreaths adorning the walls, while around the windows were heavy masses of dark green foliage, and in the baptismal font bloomed a magnificent calla lily" (*Union and Record*, December 28, 1877). Shortly afterward, however, Rev. Karcher left Calvary for the Roman Catholic priesthood.

The Rev. Charles T. Coer, Dec. 1, 1878 to March 1, 1882

The Rev. Charles Coer came to Rochester from Shakopee with the mission churches at Kasson and Elgin under his care. A new altar and reredos on the wall above the altar were installed in 1880, and a black walnut pulpit was placed on the west wall. After his resignation on March 1, 1882, Rev. Coer brought from New York City fifty young Englishmen to learn American farming methods, placing them on farms around Rochester. By December Mr. Coer was adjudged insane and committed to the State Hospital for treatment before he returned to the state of New York.

Calvary Church had no rector from March 1, 1882 to May 1, 1884

Bishop Whipple provided students and faculty from Seabury Divinity School in Faribault. Meanwhile, Rochester was devastated by the tornado of August 21, 1883. Parish organizations continued to minister to the parish and to the city struggling to rebuild.

The Rev. R.N. Avery, May 1, 1884 to June 1, 1888

The Rev. R.N. Avery and his wife moved into the first rectory the wardens and vestry had built on lots joining the church property in 1885. He had come from Sandusky, Ohio, with a family. During his tenure, the oil-burning lamps over the center aisle were replaced by kerosene chandeliers. For four years Calvary had a stable and active church life under the guidance of Rev. Avery.

The Rev. A.R. Taylor, June 1, 1888 to April 16, 1889

The Rev. A.R. Taylor's brief ministry was marked by "sociables" at the homes of J.E. Judd, William W. Mayo, and H.C. Butler, as well as by fundraisers sponsored by the parish ladies. At his resignation Rev. Taylor moved to St. John's Church, Mankato, Minnesota. The wardens and vestry had, however, offered the position of rector to the Rev. William W. Fowler on April 1, 1889.

The Rev. William W. Fowler, April 1, 1889 to Jan. 1, 1912

The memorial window at Calvary's entrance is the tribute of the parish to this distinguished rector. Depicting Rev. Fowler preaching to Native Americans seated around him, the window represents his work among the Dakota as well as the esteem in which he was held by Calvary and the Rochester community. The window was a gift to Calvary in 1950 from Rev. Fowler's sons.

Born in Little Falls, New York, William W. Fowler was ordained deacon and priest in Nebraska to work among the Dakota at Canton, South Dakota, and the Santee reservation. Bishop Whipple brought him to Minnesota where he was assistant to the rector at Gethsemane, Minneapolis. He accepted the position at Calvary on April 1, 1889. The Rev. Charles Kite served as his assistant from 1894 to 1895, working at Chatfield and St. Charles, where he eventually moved. Rev. Fowler served Calvary for over 22 years and retired to a son's farm near Canton. Serving Holy Trinity Church, Luverne, he died in 1923 and is buried at Oakwood Cemetery, Rochester.

Rev. Fowler had a long, effective ministry, moving Calvary from a small-town congregation to a prominent parish in an increasingly thriving community. His church organizations, ministries for young people, educational programs for children, music and liturgy, building improvements and additions, administration, ecclesial, and financial expertise all mark an outstanding period of growth and prosperity in Calvary's history.

The Rev. Arthur Hunter Wurtele, Jan. 1, 1912 to May 1, 1925

The Rev. Arthur H. Wurtele guided Calvary Church through World War I and into the prosperous 1920s. He came to Rochester from Trinity Church in Duluth, where he had been rector and then dean when the parish was made the Pro-Cathedral. He was a Canadian and the son of a clergyman. While at Calvary he also served Chatfield, Rushford, and Mantorville and was faithful in visiting the hospitals in the growing medical community. Rev. Wurtele was involved in many parish and community activities, especially Troop 1 of the Boy Scouts, the Boy's Brigade (choir boys), the St. Andrew's Brotherhood, the Girls' Friendly Society, and the Minnesota Symphony Orchestra concerts in Rochester. He also served as chaplain to the Home Guards.

During Rev. Wurtele's tenure, Calvary had its first parish secretary and the brief assistance of the Rev. J. Ross Colquhoun, who continued his own ministry at Chatfield and Rushford. A new rectory and parish hall were built on the adjoining lots and improvements made to the existing buildings. His ministry was a period of substance and community involvement during a time when Mayo Clinic was beginning to establish itself as a world leader in medicine.

The Rev. William Wesley Daup, May 1, 1925 to May 31, 1926

The one-year ministry of Rev. Daup at Calvary was a time of conflict, dissension, and diocesan disagreement after which the wardens and vestry sought his dismissal.

The Rev. Guy Clifton Menefee, Sept. 15, 1926 to Oct. 1, 1954

The Rev. Guy C. Menefee was born in Albert Lea in 1886 and received degrees from the University of Minnesota and Seabury Divinity School in Faribault. Proficient in languages, he taught New Testament and Greek at Seabury while serving parishes in Owatonna and Northfield. In 1934, when Seabury Divinity School merged with Western Theological Seminary and moved to Evanston, Illinois, Seabury-Western awarded Rev. Menefee an honorary Doctor of Divinity.

Dr. Menefee and his family moved from the rectory beside Calvary Church in 1932 to a home in a residential neighborhood at 1150 First Street SW. When he retired, he moved to Wadena, Minnesota, where he served several congregations until his final illness. At his death in 1958, he was buried at Oakwood Cemetery in Rochester.

His 28-year ministry at Calvary was marked by financial stability and a healthy infrastructure of parish organizations and activities. With growing numbers of patients at the Mayo Clinic, the diocese decided to free Calvary's rector of hospital chaplaincy responsibilities by funding a full-time hospital chaplaincy. The Rev. G.L. Brown served in that capacity from 1931 to 1946, followed by the Rev. Leslie Hallett from 1946 to 1965.

In addition, during Dr. Menefee's tenure several modifications and additions were made to the buildings to accommodate parish growth. In particular, the old rectory, which had been the home of the hospital chaplains, was modified for use as Sunday School and office space. The lych-gate was built to shelter the main entrance to Calvary. During Dr. Menefee's ministry, the parish grew from 550 baptized members to 1,100, stretching the facility at its downtown location.

The Rev. O. Wendell McGinnis, Oct. 1, 1954 to Aug. 7, 1965

The Rev. O. Wendell McGinnis was born in Tiffin, Ohio, in 1908, and received degrees from Kenyon College and Bexley Hall. He was ordained deacon in 1934 and priest in 1935 in the Diocese of Ohio. After serving there, he accepted the position of rector at St. Paul's, Duluth, in 1943.

On October 1, 1954, he and his wife, Charlotte, and their family came to Rochester and moved into a newly purchased rectory at 717

Memorial Pkwy. SW. He knew at the outset that Calvary had outgrown its downtown facilities and that the parish programs had outgrown the ministry of one rector. From 1956 to 1959, Frances Reynolds assisted Rev. McGinnis in Christian Education. She held a Master of Religious Education degree from Union Theological Seminary in New York.

From 1959 to 1962, the Rev. Peter Paulson was director of Christian Education at Calvary with responsibilities for pastoral care in anticipation of an expanded parish program. The Sunday School enrolled 375 children, taught by 34 teachers. Calvary's baptized membership was 1,400. When Rev. Paulson resigned in 1962 to continue a mission in Nigeria, the Rev. Robert Fenwick accepted the position. He and Rev. McGinnis coordinated the move of the congregation between the new parochial mission of St. Luke's and the old downtown parish. On December 15, 1963, Rev. Fenwick accepted the position of rector at the new St. Luke's Church.

Rev. McGinnis' health began to fail with terminal cancer, with death coming quickly on August 7, 1965. He is buried, as are three of his predecessors, at Oakwood Cemetery in Rochester.

Wendell McGinnis' remarkable ministry at Calvary guided the Episcopalian community in Rochester through the difficult transition of outgrowing the downtown facility, making decisions among several alternative sites, and dividing the community into two congregations. A capable and focused leader, he sustained a neutral and healing course through the transition.

The Rev. Samuel W. Cook, Oct. 27, 1965 to Jan. 1, 1986

Born in Minneapolis, the Rev. Samuel W. Cook received degrees from

Macalester College in St. Paul and Seabury-Western Theological Seminary in Evanston, Illinois. His entire ministry was in the Diocese of Minnesota. Known as "Sam" to his parishioners, he served St. Martin's-by-the-Lake, Minnetonka, and St. Mary's in St. Paul, before accepting the position at Calvary.

With St. Luke's Episcopal Church attracting Calvary's younger families as well as new families moving to Rochester, Rev. Cook's initial task was challenging. In focusing Calvary's programs on mission and outreach, he moved the parish out of itself into pastoral concern for Mayo Clinic patients and outreach for those in need around the world. From July 1, 1982, to July 31, 1984, Rev. Cook was assisted by the ministry of a curate, the Rev. Lawrence Bussey, and his wife, Meg. Rev. Cook oversaw significant alterations and construction, from the building of Sunday School classrooms to the construction of the columbarium, ambulatory, and educational-office building. In 1978, the Rochester flood severely damaged the Memorial Parkway rectory as well as the Cooks' personal possessions, so a new rectory was purchased at 1012 Northern Heights Dr. NE.

Rev. Cook announced his resignation effective December 31, 1985, and the wardens and vestry granted him a three-month sabbatical on October 1, 1985. At the end of his twenty-year ministry, the parish had grown to a baptized membership of 760 and was debt-free and well-endowed.

The Rev. Nicklas A. Mezacapa, Sept. 1, 1986, to present

Born in Cleveland, Ohio, on February 5, 1949, the Rev. Nicklas A. Mezacapa received degrees from Heidelberg College and Colgate-Rochester/Bexley Hall/Crozer Seminary, and was ordained deacon in 1981 and priest in 1982.

Known to his parishioners as "Father Nick," he and his wife, Edna, and their two daughters came to Calvary from St. John's, Cedar Rapids, Iowa, having served as well at St. Luke's in Kalamazoo, Michigan. The wardens and vestry had sold the rectory that had been purchased for the Cook family, giving the Mezacapas the alternative of purchasing their own home, which they did.

Photo by Curt Sanders

The Rev. Nicklas A. Mezacapa

The church was nestled in the complex of the Mayo Medical Center in downtown Rochester, which by the late 1980s was drawing tens of thousands of patients from around the world. Under Father Nick's guidance, Calvary focused first on increasing its ministry to children and young people, thereby attracting more young families, and then on becoming an oasis of healing and pastoral care in the larger community. Renovating and expanding the educational facilities on the building's north side, Calvary opened an entrance on the park overlooking the recently completed Gonda Building at Mayo Clinic. With new meeting rooms, an elevator, and freshly landscaped grounds, the entire facility became a sacred place for solace and healing, serving a diverse congregation in an urban setting.

At the same time, Calvary worked to define its mission through a series of self-studies, parish retreats, and focus groups. These resulted in a vision statement and subsequently, a new mission statement: "to cultivate the God-given gifts of all in order to share the living water of the Calvary oasis." It became clear during this self-analysis that the parish was moving from the traditional smaller pastoral church model toward a programmatic model in which the leadership is more widely spread among the members of the congregation.

As a result, the parish reorganized into four "core" administrative groups which facilitated lay leadership in directing the parish's work and mission. The Worship Core includes music, all the service groups that assist with worship, and seasonal festivals and dinners. The Faith Formation Core includes Sunday School and adult education, the nursery, youth groups, and small study groups. The Service Core is responsible for all outreach and mission work, as well as "in-house" pastoral and newcomer visitations and fellowship. And lastly, the Administration Core oversees work related to finances, such as stewardship and planned giving, and maintains the church building, garden, columbarium, and archives. It also includes both the personnel and technology committees. Each core has a volunteer chair, who works as a team member with the staff person for that area. Core meetings are held once a month and include representatives from the wardens and vestry.

Thus, in its 150th year, Calvary found itself with a new administrative organization aimed at not just meeting the parish's own needs but also helping the congregation connect with the wider community. In this endeavor Calvary is blessed to have Father Nick. With his spiritual gifts as a preacher, his community theatre performances, and his inspirational presentations to health care workers, patients, and others locally and nationwide, "Father Nick" is well-known as the energetic and inspired pastor of the "little brick church across from the Mayo Clinic."

The Ministry of Deacons at Calvary

During the Reformation, the Church of England retained the order of deacons to serve with priests and bishops in the ordained ministry. Like their pre-Reformation counterparts, deacons served for one year in transition to the priesthood. In the 19th century, the order was revived as a permanent ministry under the direction of the bishop. A deacon was assigned social and pastoral functions in a parish church and mentored by the rector.

This non-salaried ministry was open only to men. A separate order of female deaconesses served under the direction of bishops as lay persons with social ministries. In the Diocese of Minnesota, deaconesses took on a leadership role in Native American reservation ministries and in work among the elderly. In 1976, when the Episcopal Church began admitting women to the three orders of deacon, priest, and bishop, many existing deaconesses chose to be ordained. Deacons today carry the title "the Reverend" and wear the stole across the left shoulder during liturgical services. They continue to serve without salary.

Photo by Bill Charboneau

The Rev. Ginny Padzieski, deacon.

Calvary's pastoral and social-action ministries have been greatly enriched by three members who prepared for and received ordination as deacons: the Rev. Edward "Jed" Harris (1977-1990); the Rev. Donald Twentyman (1982-1993); and the Rev. Virginia "Ginny" Padzieski (1992-present). Since 2005, Rev. Padzieski has also served as Calvary's Director of Christian Education. She is the first ordained woman to serve the parish.

The Rev. Donald Twentyman and the Rev. Edward R. "Jed" Harris, deacons

For ye are all the children of God by faith in Christ Jesus
1828 Jane T Graham 1896 ✝ 1822 Joseph Graham ✝✝✝

66

Chapter 5

Children and Youth

By Barbara Toman

Anyone who enters Calvary Episcopal Church is immediately drawn to the beautiful stained-glass window above the altar. Rendered by Tiffany in glowing red and blue, in soft greens and tans and pink, it shows Jesus surrounded by children: "For ye are all children of God by faith in Christ Jesus" (Galatians 3:26, KJV).

Generations of Calvary children have whiled away the service staring at that window. Alan Ackerman remembers doing so in the 1940s, especially on Christmas Eve when he snuggled up against his grandmother's sealskin coat to keep warm. "As a child, I identified with Jesus wanting to be around the children, and vice versa," Al says. "And when I was older, the Communion of Saints entered my mind."

It was a natural thought progression for a boy with deep roots in the parish. The altar window was a gift in 1904 from Al's great-uncle, Dr. Christopher Graham, and his great-aunt, Edith Graham Mayo, in honor of their parents. A life-long member of Calvary, Al recalls as a teenager volunteering to acolyte at 8:00, so he could race home on his bike and have the funny papers to himself while the rest of the family worshiped at 9:30. He and his wife, Shirley, raised four children at Calvary; Al taught church school for twenty years. "I remember a lot of my own Sunday School teachers being inspired in some way," he says. "I wanted to do the same thing, to form a relationship with the kids. They were *my* kids."

That feeling—that they are all our kids—is shared by many at Calvary. The altar window is the most visible outward sign of a deep commitment to children, dating back virtually to the parish's founding.

The First Sunday School

Soon after arriving in 1867, Calvary's second rector, the Rev. William J. Johnstone, organized a Sunday School for the new parish. Among the early teachers was the redoubtable Margaret Brackenridge, after whom Brackenridge Hall is named. Mrs. Brackenridge almost certainly was Calvary's longest-serving teacher, retiring just a few years before her death in 1914 at the age of 84. She taught the "infant class," or kindergarten and younger students. The older children were separated into a girls' and a boys' class, taught respectively in the early years by Abbie Faitoute and Mrs. H.C. Butler.

It's impossible to say for certain what those early students learned, as no accounts were kept of Sunday School activities. They must have been an active group, however, for parish records indicate substantial gifts to the church from the Sunday School.

Calvary, in turn, seems to have set a high priority on its children's needs. The parish's first hall, known as "The Guild Hall," was built in 1891, primarily to accommodate the growing Sunday School. Construction was requested by the Ladies Parish Aid Society, an

GIFTS TO CALVARY FROM THE SUNDAY SCHOOL

1868:
Bishop's chair in the chancel made of black walnut, and bench for clergy.

1871:
White stone baptismal font.

1879:
Black walnut pulpit.

1884:
New chandeliers in the nave of the church.

organization founded in 1860 and originally named "The Sewing Society of Calvary Church."

By 1900, Calvary's Sunday School had grown to 73 pupils and nine teachers. The parish archives have a few children's worship-service leaflets from that era. "A Sunday School Flower Service," dated May 21, 1900, follows the Morning Prayer format with hymns and Scripture that mention flowers ("Lo! The winter is past. The flowers appear on the earth" [Song of Solomon 2:11-12] and "Consider the lilies of the field, how they grow" [Matthew 6:28]). A 1909 bulletin titled "A Sunday School Service for Easter" indicates the common practice of children worshiping separately from adults.

Amid rapid parish growth in that era, Calvary launched efforts that look a bit like today's youth groups. In 1894, the Rev. William Wallace Fowler formed a "Young Peoples Society for Spiritual Growth." It may have been aimed more at young adults, however, as a few of the female members are listed as "Mrs." After its organization the group isn't mentioned much in parish records.

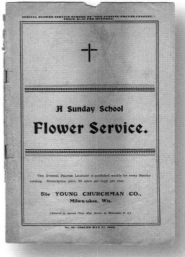

A children's service bulletin dated 1900

An Early Youth Group

Calvary's second attempt at a "youth group" had a bit more traction. In 1912, Mr. Fowler's successor, the Rev. Arthur Hunter Wurtele, organized "The Young Peoples Guild of Calvary Episcopal Church." A book with notes beautifully handwritten by the group's secretary, Rodney Waldron, survives. The thoroughness of the young people's planning is impressive; the "Constitution and By Laws" ran to five pages. For four months the group was very active, hosting parties and raising money for charity (for more on the group, see Chapter 14).

But after Christmas 1912, the Guild doesn't seem to have met regularly. It was reorganized the following year into two separate groups, one for young men and another for young women. The men's group is never mentioned again. The women's group took the name "St. Margaret's Guild"; its occasional minutes concern mostly social events. In 1915, the secretary, Louise Butler, wrote: "On May 5th, we enjoyed a most delightful evening at the Misses Willson's at Red Oaks. Thirty-five were present to participate in the games and sociability of the evening and a collection of $3.00 helped enhance the treasury." By 1919, the listed members of St. Margaret's Guild were all married women, taking on such tasks as sewing choir vestments and conducting rummage and bake sales.

As St. Margaret's Guild matured in membership and tasks, the parish youth had other options. Soon after coming to Calvary, Rev. Wurtele started a chapter of the Girls' Friendly Society (the organization, founded in England in 1875 and in the U.S. in 1877, still exists. It is somewhat similar to Girl Scouts, but affiliated with the Episcopal Church). Calvary's Girls' Friendly Society must have been fairly active; in 1914, it presented a set of purple altar hangings to the new Altar Guild. In 1923, the Old Rectory (located north of the church, and demolished in 1962) was renovated for use by the Girls' Friendly Society.

Calvary also had scouting troops. Rev. Wurtele started a Boy Scout troop in the parish in 1915, and served as scoutmaster. Under the Rev. Guy C. Menefee, who became rector in 1926, Calvary sponsored both a Boy Scout and a Girl Scout troop.

Standing-Room-Only Christmas Pageants

The activities of Calvary's Sunday School and youth groups become clearer after Easter 1938, when the parish began publishing the *Visitor* newsletter. At that point the Church School had 127 students (73 girls and 54 boys) and eleven teachers. The newsletter, written by Rev. Menefee until his retirement in 1954, carried regular updates on Church School and youth projects.

One of the first items concerns the Lenten "mite boxes" in which Church School students collected coins for a special Easter offering. In 1940, donations totaled $75. "This offering has been devoted to work among children in various parts of the world since its inception in 1877, and deserves the moral backing of every one of us," Rev. Menefee wrote in the *Visitor.* In addition, every Christmas the students collected clothing, books, and toys for the Ojibwe reservations at White Earth or Leech Lake.

The high point of the Church School year seems to have been the annual Christmas pageant, presented on or near Christmas Eve with the Junior Choir providing music. Participants brought wrapped gifts which were given to the Salvation Army for distribution to needy families. The pageant was so popular that dozens of people were turned away for lack of space. Writing in the *Visitor* about the 1939 pageant, Rev. Menefee noted: "Every available square inch of space was in use, chairs even having to be placed inside the sanctuary rails to accommodate ten of the smaller choir members. It is unfortunate that our space is so limited that only a small part of the Parish can attend the pageant." Only illness could keep the crowd away; in 1943, half the Sunday School students had 'flu or measles and missed the pageant.

Another popular event in the '40s and '50s was Anna Pemberton's annual presentation of the Easter story. While telling it, she would place hand-painted figures on a flannel board as illustration. Al Ackerman remembers particularly the moment when the empty tomb was discovered. "The sky was purple, and the red-caped Roman centurions with their silver helmets stood on the lush green grass," he says. "And then the amazing stone rolled away. Mrs. Pemberton could keep the entire Sunday School entranced."

As for youth groups, the *Visitor* also reported regularly on the "Young People's Fellowship," or Y.P.F., which consisted mostly of high-school students but at times included those in junior high and college. The Y.P.F. had periodic fundraisers, such as an annual ice-cream social (the one on St. Patrick's Day 1946 charged 25 cents admission and netted $50). Proceeds went to the diocese's fund for renovating its Cass Lake property as a conference and retreat center. The fundraising by Calvary's Y.P.F. and similar branches elsewhere in Minnesota paid off; by 1952, Cass Lake camp was open for summer sessions.

Other Calvary youth fundraisers benefited post-war Europe. In December 1947, the youth collected twenty boxes of clothing, weighing more than 400 pounds, to ship to devastated areas.

Youth Worship Services and Square Dancing

From the 1930s into the 1950s, Calvary also had an annual "Young People's Service," conducted entirely by the youth. Initially, it was held in the afternoon of the Sunday nearest All Saints; in later years it was a "Festival of Light" on a Sunday afternoon during Epiphany. Although the entire parish was invited, the services apparently were attended mostly by the youth and their parents. Rev. Menefee believed the occasions deserved "a far larger recognition" from the congregation: "These high school boys and girls are tomorrow's parish," he wrote in November 1945. "They need encouragement and a feeling that they are a part of the parish now."

The youth had plenty of picnics and social events -- square-dancing in Brackenridge was popular on Friday evenings during the mid-1950s – but they also listened to guest lectures on some pretty cosmopolitan topics. In March 1953, Mabel Tow, a parishioner born in China who was doing post-graduate work in anesthesia at Mayo, "told the Y.P.F. group something of Christian work in her homeland before the advent of the present regime," Rev. Menefee wrote in the *Visitor*. "She referred also to some of the changes effected since the Communists came into control." In January 1960, the newsletter reported that a Parish Youth Supper included a talk on "the meaning of Judaism, by Rabbi Schacter of B'Nai B'Rith Center."

Other topics were more mundane. In May 1960, Mr. and Mrs. Everett Klampe hosted a meeting for the junior- and senior-high groups that featured a movie called "Getting Along with Parents," followed by discussion.

Classes in the Kitchen, the Basement, Wherever

With Calvary growing rapidly after World War II, the Church School suffered a serious space crunch. There was no education wing. Since 1867, classes had met in any available room. Starting in the mid-1940s, Rev. Menefee gathered with parents and teachers every autumn to

Sunday School, 1953. This class met in the sexton's house just north of the church. Originally built as a rectory, the house was demolished in 1962.

choreograph a complicated dance: deciding where classes should be held, and what if any portion of the worship service children of various ages should attend. (Sunday School and worship times overlapped.)

In the September 28, 1945, *Visitor*, Rev. Menefee outlined a plan that involved various classes meeting in the basement, Brackenridge Hall, the church kitchen, the music director's studio, the sexton's sitting room, and the Memorial room in Brackenridge Hall. Meanwhile, depending on their age, students were either to go to Church School immediately or attend the first part of the service before "withdrawing" to class. "A considerable number of parents and teachers have had a share in setting up the new plan," Rev. Menefee noted, "but even so, it is too much to hope it can start off altogether smoothly."

Apparently, he was right. In the next newsletter, Rev. Menefee said it was "obvious" that having "all children above first graders come into the church would not work." (Sunday School wasn't the only victim of overcrowding; services themselves were packed. It wasn't uncommon for 200 people to be turned away on Christmas Eve.) Plan B called for second, third and fourth graders to have their own service in Brackenridge Hall before going to their classrooms. Succeeding newsletters included pleas for more teachers, to allow them to alternate Sundays between teaching and worshiping.

The following year, 1946, was especially challenging. With enrollment still growing, Rev. Menefee decided to split the Sunday School. Nursery through fourth grade would have class at 11 a.m. "Seventh and eighth grade people will report at nine-thirty as there will be no room to accommodate them at eleven o'clock." Grades five and six would attend the 9:30 service "and withdraw for instruction during the second canticle at morning prayer or during the hymn before the sermon at Holy Communion." (In those days Holy Communion was done only once a month; the congregation had Morning Prayer on the other Sundays.)

Kindergarten Sunday School class, 1953. The class met in Brackenridge Hall.

To top it all off, because of post-war austerity, some of the classroom materials hadn't arrived. "The paper shortage is still very real," Rev. Menefee wrote, "and it is altogether possible some groups will be without material or will be only partially supplied."

The split schedule proved tough on families with children in both age groups. In 1951, the church went back to a single "Family Worship" at 9:30 a.m. "With all classes meeting at one time, attendance at church will be much easier for many people who formerly had to get one or more children to each of the Church School sessions," Rev. Menefee wrote. But within a month, the Church School teachers were meeting to discuss the resulting overcrowding.

"The Real Answer"-- A New Building

Two new youth groups were highlighted in the May 15, 1961, issue of the *Visitor*. In the "music appreciation group" led by Peter Carryer and Dr. Preston Manning, "selected recordings" were played, "followed by discussion and fellowship." The "literature appreciation group" started by John Vaughn and Dr. J. William McRoberts, had "selected the prize-winning novel of Ernest Hemingway, *For Whom the Bell Tolls*, for analysis and discussion from a Christian perspective."

Six years later, the Nov. 15, 1967 *Visitor* announced the topic for an upcoming meeting of the junior- and senior-high youth: "Let's Talk about Hippies and Drugs." According to the newsletter, "Mr. Link from the Juvenile Department will speak. Role play and discussion! Refreshments."

For Rev. Menefee there was only one solution: "The real answer must wait upon the erection of a building to give adequate space for Church School as well as other activities." A planning committee was organized in 1952. Fundraising started two years later, but was soon called off amid talk that the building might be sold and a new church built outside downtown.

As a short-term solution, the parish renovated the Old Rectory (where the Girls' Friendly Society had met) to provide classrooms for grades 5 through 9. Calvary's nursery also was founded at this time. In 1953, members of the Helen B. Judd Group, a women's group, organized babysitting in a room above the church secretary's office during the 9:30 and 11:00 services.

But the Church School just kept growing. In 1956, two years after Dr. Menefee's retirement, Calvary hired Frances Reynolds as its first paid director of education. The 9:30 service was moved back to 9:15, to allow more time for Church School. Writing in the *Visitor*, the new rector, the Rev. O. Wendell McGinnis, promised "well-organized classes with splendid courses of instruction and excellent teachers for all children from the age of 3 through ninth grade."

By 1957, the Church School had 312 students, nearly double the enrollment twenty years earlier. With the vestry expressing concern about the fire hazard posed by extra chairs placed in the church at 9:15, childless adults were urged to worship at 8:00 or 11:00. That apparently didn't work. In 1958, the Church School again was split between the 9:15 and 11 a.m. services. Families were asked to notify the church of which service they would attend, and to do so consistently.

That was the year in which, following a suggestion from Bishop Keeler, Calvary decided to establish a parochial mission in northwest Rochester, which eventually became St. Luke's. In retrospect, it was a high-water time for the Episcopal Church. National membership hit a record 3.27 million. (The all-time high was 3.6 million members in 1965. In 2008, membership totaled about 2.2 million.) By 1959, Calvary's Church School had ballooned to 375 students and 34 teachers. Classes continued meeting during the summer as well as during the regular school year. A two-week Vacation Bible School also was offered in August. Miss Reynolds had resigned to take a job in California, and the vestry hired the Rev. Peter H. Paulson to serve as associate rector and Christian Education director. He resigned in 1962 to take a job as principal of a secondary school in rural Nigeria.

A "Gray" Parish, Overnight

The effort to build the mission church was fueled by families with young children, who wanted more space for a Christian Education program. For two years after the mission church's completion, it operated in tandem with Calvary. Church School was offered at both locations, with a total enrollment of 429 students in 1962. Youngsters aged 3 through 5 attended a children's worship service; older children attended part of the regular service, then went to class. A single Christmas pageant was held at the mission church.

The following autumn, the vestry voted to establish the mission church as a separate parish, named "St. Luke's." Parishioners were urged to choose which parish to affiliate with. The Rev. Robert Fenwick, Rev. Paulson's successor as Calvary's associate rector and Christian Education director, was called to be rector of St. Luke's.

PAGEANT
MAYHEM

Pageants are unpredictable. One at Calvary in the mid-1960s dissolved into mayhem when the girls playing the Virgin Mary and Joseph got the giggles and couldn't utter a single line. A Tiny Tears doll represented baby Jesus, and Bette Dines recalls her ten-year-old daughter (who was Mary) "standing there at the altar, dangling this Tiny Tears doll by the leg" while the congregation joined in the laughter. That night, the Rev. Sam Cook phoned to reassure the Dines that it was the best Christmas Eve pageant Calvary ever had.

By 1965, Calvary had "just a handful of children," according to the parish history published in 1985. They were taught by the Rev. Samuel Wainwright Cook, who became rector in 1965 following Rev. McGinnis' retirement and death. Classes met in the Old Rectory.

About a year after Rev. Cook's arrival, the vestry voted to spend $190,000 to build eleven classrooms in a new education wing as well as new offices and an apartment for the sexton. The Old Rectory was razed, and construction of the addition began in January 1968. By the time the project was finished, the cost had grown to $210,000, of which $125,000 was raised by the parish. (The debt remained until 1977.) The new structure was dedicated February 3, 1969.

Finding children to fill those new classrooms took some time. "For many years when young families would visit Calvary, they would look around and say, 'It seems like this is primarily a congregation for the elderly,'" says Kay Karsell, who moved to Rochester with her young family in 1968. "It was many years getting a young community developed at Calvary."

In 1975, average Sunday School attendance was 61 students, according to Calvary's annual report. Students continued to collect money in Lenten mite boxes. Vacation Bible School was offered most summers, in conjunction with St. Luke's. The senior-high youth group continued to host the annual Shrove Tuesday pancake supper, went canoeing and skiing in Wisconsin, and held bake sales with proceeds financing youth retreats.

Around 1977, some youth began to attend TEC ("Teens Encounter Christ") weekends. In the September *Visitor* that year, students in grades 10 through 12 were invited to a session at St. Stephen's-Edina. The

ENVIRONMENTAL EDUCATION IN THE '70s

On Nov. 21, 1976, the seventh- and eighth-grade Sunday School class taught the adult class, using materials and ideas from their own curriculum on "Man's Relationship with God's Creation." They asked the adults questions about environmental issues, then split with them into small groups to discuss Genesis 1 and "what man's response and relationship to God's Creation should be," according to the *Visitor*. Afterwards, the youth were asked what they had learned from teaching the adults.

Their answers:

"1. Adults do not come when they are called.

"2. Adults do not always follow directions.

"3. Adults do not raise their hands to be called upon."

weekend would include short talks by clergy and young people, as well as worship and recreation. "No one has ever left the weekend sorry they had come," the newsletter said. "You will make many new friends, and get to know God much better, too."

A Shot of Energy

Calvary's education and youth programs were greatly energized in 1982 by the arrival of the Rev. Larry Bussey and his wife, Meg. Larry served as assistant rector and education director. He and Meg started an Education for Ministry group at Calvary, as well as revising the Sunday School curriculum. They organized hayrides, pizza and movie parties, and trips to Minneapolis to, among other things, see *A Christmas Carol* at the Guthrie Theatre. The Busseys left Rochester in 1984 when Larry was called to be assistant to the rector at St. Martin's-Minnetonka Beach.

Under the Rev. Nicklas A. Mezacapa, who became Calvary's rector in 1986, the parish set out to become a "spiritual oasis" in downtown Rochester. For children and youth, Calvary sought to provide a place where they might experience the living waters of our faith through vibrant educational programs. To that end some long-standing Calvary traditions were tweaked.

In 1998, the Christmas Eve pageant was moved to Epiphany Sunday, serving as the homily at the 9:00 and 11:00 services. For the children, it was an opportunity to lead in worship and to feel included; for adults, it was a chance to experience the faith through young eyes. A new version of the pageant was presented in 1999 under the direction of Nancy Malloy, who was hired as Christian Education director the previous autumn. Telling the nativity story from the Annunciation to the arrival of the wise men, the pageant reaches its climax with the entrance of a papier-mâché camel, festooned with gold beads and false eyelashes.

Although Nancy spent just two years at Calvary, she had a major impact on the education program. She introduced simple but liturgically instructive customs such as the Alleluia banners – rolls of paper decorated by students, hidden in the undercroft on the last Sunday of Epiphany, then "resurrected" and carried into church on Easter morning. "This teaches the season of the church," Nancy wrote in the *Visitor*, "and also teaches the children to wait."

During Lent 1999, the Sunday School teachers decided to have students raise money for Heifer Project International, a group that donates

livestock to needy people in the U.S. and abroad. The initial goal was to raise $120 to "buy" a goat. By April, the Sunday School had raised $450—nearly enough for four sheep. "The teachers came up with the idea of mission," Nancy wrote in the *Visitor*. "But the kids are the ones who have surprised us. Now we, the adults

involved, are in awe of their energy and enthusiasm." By Easter, the students had raised $600, enough for five sheep.

But the fifth-grade class wanted more. They insisted on raising $5,000 to buy an "ark," or a pair of every sort of animal Heifer provides. Calling themselves "The Children of Christ," they formed a youth group for grades five through eight that held bake sales, car washes and a "hunger meal". By Lent 2000, with some help from Calvary's social action committee, the youth met their goal.

Bolstered by this energy, Calvary's Sunday School entered a period of growth. The Oasis building project included a bright new nursery and better facilities for the younger students. In 2005, Calvary's deacon, the Rev. Ginny Padzieski, became Director of Education; under her leadership Calvary has maintained its recent traditions of team teaching, an annual St. Nicholas party for younger students, and a Festival of Faith that concludes the Sunday School year. She also adopted a new curriculum based on "core" Bible stories and concepts of the Episcopal faith, aimed at giving young people the

Photos by Cara Edwards

Mission trip to Bay St. Louis, Mississippi, June 2008. Leah Beltz and Claire Richer help tear down a house that was ruined by Hurricane Katrina.

Photo by Mark Williams

knowledge, reflective tools and sense of community they need to live their faith daily.

A New Focus on Service

For many young people, living the faith daily means working together on service projects. In the spring of 2004, six high-school students spent a week in New York City, where among other efforts they worked in a soup kitchen. The trip was so successful that the parish committed to undertaking a youth mission trip every other year. In summer 2006, six high-school students spent a week at Cass Lake Episcopal Camp—the same camp funded by the old Young People's Fellowship in the 1950s—clearing woodland paths and learning about Ojibwe culture.

Two years later, spurred by a desire to help with Hurricane Katrina cleanup and rebuilding, the youth decided to raise $12,000 to travel to an Episcopal mission in Bay St. Louis, Mississippi. They succeeded; and in June 2008, thirteen youths and five adults made the trip to the Gulf Coast. Before flying home, they spent a day in New Orleans looking at hurricane damage and listening to jazz.

The following September, on Holy Cross Day, the youth led all three morning services. The students wrote prayers based on their mission experience, engaged in a dialogue with Father Nick as part of the homily, and presented jazz and gospel hymns during the regular Sunday morning worship. It was, perhaps, reminiscent of the "Young People's Services" sixty years earlier, but this time, the pews were full.

A D D E N D U M

Early Teachers

Several pillars of Calvary parish, some of them connected to Mayo Clinic, taught Sunday School in the 19th century. Most of them were multi-taskers:

- Emma F. Judd, the mother of Dr. E. Starr Judd and C.M. Judd, was also organist and choir director from 1871-75, as well as secretary and treasurer of the Parish Aid Society.

- Blanche Graham (Margaret Brackenridge's daughter) and her husband, Dr. Christopher Graham, the second partner to join the Mayo brothers' practice.

- Dr. A.F. Kilbourne, who came to Rochester in the late 19th century to supervise a new psychiatric hospital. Serving as well on the vestry and as senior warden, he taught the "older boys" class.

- Miss Laura and Miss Emily Willson. Their father, C.C. Willson, helped Frank B. Kellogg study law. Kellogg, who grew up in Rochester, served as ambassador to Britain and Secretary of State and was awarded the Nobel Peace Prize in 1929.

The Forum, meeting in Crawford Hall, 2009.

Chapter 6

Faith Formation:
Adult Education at Calvary

Contributors: Nancy Haworth Dingel, Dottie Hawthorne, Martha Mangan, Julie Roenigk, and Barbara Toman

Mindful of the promise we make in the Baptismal Covenant to "continue in the apostles' teaching," Calvary Episcopal Church has always offered opportunities for adult education. The format and topics have varied widely. Like fashion, education tends to run in cycles, with a particular sort of class becoming popular for a time before something new springs up in its place. Over the years, adult education at Calvary has included various small groups such as Lenten study groups, prayer groups, Parable Studies, Journeys in Faith, Education for Ministry, Frontiers of Faith, and Confirmation and Enquirers' classes, all of which require a commitment of attendance from members. It has also included more open formats such as the Forum which takes place between services on two Sundays a month. The common thread from Calvary's early history through today has been extending beyond formal worship services to meet the spiritual and informational needs of parishioners. Here, we offer a snapshot of adult education at Calvary in the early 21st century.

Small Groups

One of the biggest developments at Calvary in the late 20th century was the start of "small groups." Small groups range in size from six to twelve people, meet twice a month and follow a very general format of study, prayer, and fellowship. They were established to foster and deepen relationships within Calvary and thus build up the Body of Christ.

The impetus for small group ministry came from a handful of parishioners who heard about it in other congregations and sought guidance in starting the ministry at Calvary. In 1993, after training in group dynamics and mentorship, three teams of leaders—Dottie and Frank Hawthorne, Julie Roenigk and Martha Mangan, and Mary Gustafson and Sarah Winters—formed groups under the umbrella title "FISH-nets" (Fellowship in Shared Homes).

Early on, Julie Roenigk described the importance of small groups in the life of Calvary as well as her own life. "Creating community is so difficult because of how busy we all are as a society. Society seduces us into believing 'busy' is good in and of itself. I believe, though, that community is vital to the growth of the church, both individual believers and the Body of Christ. I long for a place to feel free to express doubts, fears, joys, and struggles, while being encouraged to grow in my spiritual life."

While Calvary's small groups have evolved over the years, with leaders and members changing, the commitment to creating community has remained constant. Each group developed its own flavor. For example, the Wednesday Morning small group consists of mothers seeking support and guidance in their busy lives as well as spiritual growth. Other groups have grown out of members' shared experiences at

Plate 1. *Christ Blessing Little Children.* **The altar window. Tiffany Studios, 1904.**

Plate 2.
Chalice with Grapes and Ivy. West wall of the nave. Tiffany Studios, 1905.

Plate 3.
Lilies of the Field. West wall of the nave. Tiffany Studios, 1907.

Photos by Amanda Durhma

Plate 4.
Small Cross. East wall of the nave. Tiffany Studios, 1907.

Plate 5.
Native Americans Receiving the Gospel. South wall of the vestibule, 1950.

Photos by Amanda Durhman

Plate 6.
Sermon on the
Mount, 1968.

Plate 7.
*The Healing
Window.
Northwest
entrance.*
Kjerland Stained
Glass Studio,
Northfield,
Minnesota, 2007.

Photo by Amanda Durhman

Plate 8. Watercolor by Harold Crawford, showing the lancet windows by the east entrance.

Plate 9. Bench with needlepoint cover by Bette Dines, 2005.

Plate 10. Needlepoint kneelers at the altar.

Plate 11. The reredos.

Plate 12. Sunday service, summer 2009.

Photo by Penny Duffy

Plate 13. Baptismal font.

Photo by Ian Jarman

Plate 14. The Epiphany pageant, 2004.

Plate 15. Calvary fruitcake.

Photo by Cara Edwards

Photo by Bill Charboneau

Plate 16. Baptism in the Oasis Courtyard, summer 2003.

Plate 17. Chalice.

Photo by Penny Duffy

Photo by Nick Charboneau

Plate 18. Sunday School students and teachers in the courtyard, May, 2003.

Plate 19. The Motet Choir, with Brian A. Williams, 2003.

Plate 20. The lych-gate.

Plate 21. Calvary Church east entrance.

Plate 22. Calvary Church from the southwest, 2009.

Photo by Penny Duffy

Plate 24. Calvary Church, interior, 2009.

Plate 23. Calvary Church, interior, 2009. Photo by Penny Duffy

Plate 25.
The Crawford cross, southeast corner of the courtyard, 2009.

Photo by Bill Charboneau

Plate 26. Worship in the courtyard, summer 2003.

Photo by Penny Duffy

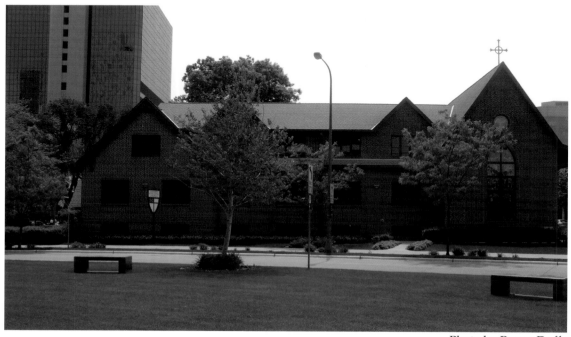

Plate 27. Calvary Church education wing, viewed from the north in 2009.

Plate 28. Oasis Courtyard, 2009. Photo by Penny Duffy

Photo by Penny Duffy

spiritual renewal events such as Cursillo. These types of groups tend to meet in members' homes and are eclectic in their reading tastes.

Other groups are more focused. The Benedictine Way is dedicated to discovering balance in life through prayer, study of the Gospels and St. Benedict's Rule, and community gathering. Calvary's Benedictine group formed in autumn 2006 and has met monthly with nine to twelve members who share, listen, and try to integrate aspects of the Benedictine monastic tradition into daily life so as to better live out the Gospel in today's challenging world.

Members of "Frontiers of Faith," launched by Phil Karsell in 2002, discuss modern theology and ethics from a critical point of view. For example, they have read and discussed Marcus Borg's *Meeting Jesus Again for the First Time*, watched Bill Moyers' televised interviews with Joseph Campbell, and examined non-canonical writings and case studies in ethics.

Journeys in Faith, another small group, studied a series of booklets on different aspects of Christianity. One booklet was read each week, and then discussed in a group setting. One of the newest forms of education that includes all ages is "Calvary Reads." Anyone who is interested reads a selected book during the winter. Then, in the spring, several groups are formed to discuss the book.

For those wishing to dive deeply into the foundations of their faith, Calvary began offering Education for Ministry (EfM) in 1999. Despite its name, EfM isn't intended for those seeking ordination. It is a distance-learning program from the University of the South in Sewanee, Tennessee, that educates the laity to carry out the ministry to which each baptized person is called. It meets every Thursday evening from September to

May. Over the years the EfM group has grown to include members of St. Luke's, St. Peter's in Kasson, and People of Hope Lutheran Church.

Small groups are now a mainstay at Calvary. Many lives have been blessed by being a part of a group committed to exploring faith and building community.

The Forum

For many Episcopalians coffee-and-donuts between Sunday services almost constitute an eighth sacrament. In the late 1970s, Calvary, like other Episcopal churches, added a twist to the traditional coffee hour: a Forum, or educational discussion hour, on certain Sundays between services. It was an opportunity for parishioners to expand their understanding of a range of issues and topics, viewed through the lens of faith. Assuming its present form in the mid-1990s, the Forum meets from 10:10 a.m. to 11:00 a.m. on the first and third Sundays of the month throughout the Sunday School year. For years the Forum was held in Brackenridge Hall alongside the coffee urn and donut platter. In 2008, the "coffee hour" remained in Brackenridge, and the Forum, along with its own coffee urn and donuts, moved into Crawford Hall which is equipped for audio-visual presentations.

Presenters at the Forum come from the congregation, the diocese, and the local community. Topics are suggested by parishioners and have run the gamut from environmental stewardship to Episcopal faith, history, and musical traditions; from volunteerism to interfaith hospitality, diversity, and discussions of non-Christian faiths; from the history of missionaries to impact of medical conditions such as Alzheimer's Disease and alcoholism; from the sense of God's majesty in the physics of star formation to the story of the Epiphany star. The Forum has also provided a useful format for updating the congregation on Calvary life, including reports from the parish's core groups, mission trips, and other endeavors.

The Forum is now richly woven into the fabric of Calvary life and, like other groups, provides an opportunity to share in fellowship and to discuss topics relevant to our Life in Christ within and beyond the borders of our parish.

Photo by Bill Charboneau

90

Chapter 7

Altar Guild

By Nancy Haworth Dingel

Members of the Altar Guild have the privilege of serving as God's housekeepers. The underlying purpose is to prepare a meal, a banquet as it were, as a tribute to God, using the best accoutrements available. Prayer and care are necessary attributes for anyone taking on this service. The goal can be lost in the mundane, everyday care of vessels, linens, supplies, and repairs, let alone human frailties. The work can be involved and sometimes frustrating, but when the goals of service to the Lord, and the rector, are kept in mind, the chores are rewarding.

The Altar Guild is a relatively new addition to parish life. In the earliest days of the Church, around 200 CE, a "sub-deacon" was responsible for care of the vessels used in the Eucharist. Later, the sacristan became responsible for everything in the church building, including all sacred vessels and cloth goods. With the rise of the monasteries, minor orders of monks cared for the churches, vestments, linens, and vessels. When the Church of England was established in the mid-1500s, the monasteries were closed. The parish clerk and clergy assumed the responsibilities of the sacristan and other duties.

Matrons and Spinsters, by Invitation Only

In the early 19th century the Oxford Movement redirected much of the Church of England toward giving the laity more of a role in the life of the Church. The Episcopal Church in this country followed suit. A parish clerk in the sacristy became superfluous, and the Altar Guild was created to assume responsibility for the care of vestments and altar goods.

Initially, members of the Altar Guilds were matrons or unmarried women of "excellent repute" who were not employed outside of their homes. An invitation was extended to those deemed qualified. And, as the intricacies and standards of care for precious metal vessels and crisply ironed fabrics were established, the procedures assumed strict protocols. Many months of training were overseen before full membership was attained.

At Calvary Episcopal Church, the Altar Guild was formed on February 27, 1912, at the request of the rector, the Rev. Arthur H. Wurtele. Just who performed the duties assumed by the Guild before that time is lost in the abyss of parish history—perhaps it was the parish clergy and their wives. Since then, Calvary has had an active Guild which was, for many years, modeled on the Victorian pattern of matrons and spinsters. Potential members had to be invited to join. There is a story about one rector's wife who had been a member of an Altar Guild in another parish. When her husband was called to Calvary, she thought she would be welcomed as a knowledgeable Altar Guild member, and dutifully attended a meeting. However, she was asked to leave because she had not been formally invited to join.

In 1912, on accepting the invitation from Calvary's Altar Guild, a woman was expected to progress through the steps of caring for linens and arranging flowers, to the offices of secretary, treasurer, sub-directress, and directress. She was also expected to hem and embroider linens that she personally laundered. As with other items, fair linens, which protect the altar, were donated and each was decorated with five crosses: one in the center and one in each corner of the altar. The position of the crosses is standard, but the style of crosses differs; the fair linen was therefore identifiable and named for the donor. During their months of training, new members of the Altar Guild were required to learn the names of the fair linens by the style of the crosses.

That first year, the Altar Guild made a set of green and then a set of white altar hangings. The following year, a set of red altar hangings was made and a set of purple hangings was presented to the Guild by the Girls' Friendly Society. A candle extinguisher was purchased. Individual members or other parishioners donated sacred vessels such as a silver ciborium, for holding the wafers, and a crystal cruet. All these items were consecrated by the bishop in 1913.

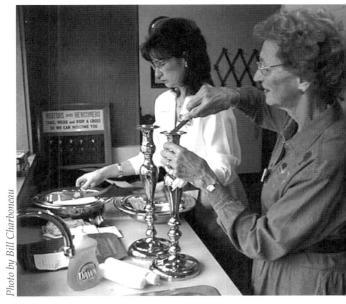

Photo by Bill Charboneau

The sacristy. Altar Guild members Cathy Charboneau and Marilyn Peck in 1997.

In the beginning an annual Guild meeting was held as close as possible to All Saints Day. A luncheon and short meeting, during which a small gold cross was presented to the retiring directress, followed this service. Attendance at monthly meetings was required.

Home-Grown Flowers; Purple Capes and Veils

As membership and duties increased, a flower calendar was established to ensure provision of flowers for each Sunday. The flowers were provided by members of the Guild from their own gardens, and also arranged by them (one wonders what flowers were available in the Minnesota winters!). After the Sunday service, the flowers were taken to shut-in parishioners by the rector or an Altar Guild member.

In the early years the Altar Guild raised funds for outreach work. From 1918 to 1923, the Guild adopted a French orphan boy. His support of $36.50 per annum was obtained through contributions, ice-cream socials, and candy sales. In addition, the Guild contributed $100 to the vestry to be applied to the church debt, and paid for a cupboard and a table to be constructed for the sacristy.

When Calvary's altar was enlarged in 1924, new linens and hangings were required. The sacristy was also remodeled at this time. In 1926, the Altar Guild assumed the responsibility of caring for the rector's vestments. Two years later, the Guild commissioned a walnut cover for the baptismal font.

By 1950, the number of Altar Guild members had reached 35. At that time, while working, Guild members wore purple capes with hairnets in the shape of a short helmet or inverted bowl. In 1951, a Junior Altar Guild was established for teenaged girls. They, too, wore the capes and head veils. Initially active only for two years, the Junior Altar Guild was re-established for several years in the 1960s.

Changes in The Book of Common Prayer in 1974 occasioned the need for different and more extensive use of the existing communion vessels, as the celebration of the Eucharist became more prevalent than Morning Prayer. Both clergy and Guild members became aware of a variety of practices that could enhance the worship service. The Altar Guild's practices have evolved over time, and frequently been altered at the direction of the incumbent rector. This is just as it should be because the rector is the ultimate leader of the Guild.

LINENS AND BIRDS AND BATS! OH MY!

Work for the Altar Guild comes with certain hazards. One Sunday in recent memory, a worker in the sacristy moved the missal desk and found a cowering brown juvenile bat. While a coworker screamed, the worker took a towel, tenderly grabbed the shaking body, and dropped it out an open window. On retrieving the towel, there was no sign of the bat. Once, a sparrow perched on the back of a pew during Sunday services. On another Sunday a bat was found sitting on the altar. With the aid of a badminton racket, it was encouraged to fly elsewhere. The next Sunday, there were two little bats perched on the altar! However, these were found to be plush replicas, purchased and placed by someone to fool her spouse!

Signs of Women's Changing Status

By the 1990s, the Altar Guild had about forty members, and that number has remained fairly constant since. The titles designated in the membership rolls are an interesting reflection of the changes in women's status over the course of the 20th century. Although the names of many early members are not recorded in the archives, those that exist are listed by "Mrs.," followed by the husband's first and last names (e.g., Mrs. John Smith). Widows retained a similar listing. Spinsters were listed as "Miss" followed by a first and last name. A divorced woman was "Mrs. Mary Smith." In the 1970s, listings for married women began to be followed by the woman's first name in parentheses (e.g., Mrs. John Smith [Mary]). In the following decade, listings had a first and last name, followed by the husband's first name (e.g., Mrs. Mary Smith [John]). Some time in the 1990s, "Mary Smith" was listed simply, with no title to designate her marital status or her husband's name.

Different Names, Constant Purpose: Calvary's St. Margaret's Altar Guild

Around the same time, Calvary's Altar Guild assumed the title "St. Margaret's Altar Guild" after St. Margaret of Scotland, a true servant of God who tirelessly labored for the Church and its people. Confusion may ensue when it is learned that another St. Margaret's Guild existed at Calvary. In 1912, under Rev. Wurtele, a Young People's Guild of Calvary Episcopal Church was formed and named "St. Margaret's Guild." Its purposes were to advance the interest of the parish and to promote sociability among the members. As with many such groups, interest waxed and waned, and around 1933 it appears to have been absorbed into the Parish Aid Society. Obviously, this guild and the current St. Margaret's

Altar Guild have never met, and their purposes are quite different.

Since naming the Altar Guild for St. Margaret, a Eucharist and the induction of new members and officers have been held on the Saturday nearest November 16, the feast day of St. Margaret of Scotland. This is followed by a luncheon to which retired and honorary Guild members are invited. At the annual Altar Guild meeting in January, a new director is presented with the traditional gold cross. Because directors may now serve for multiple years, another token of thanks is substituted for the cross in subsequent yearly meetings.

Flat Bread and Gluten-Free Wafers

In the early 2000s, traditional wafers and the "priest's host" were replaced by a more everyday type of bread. The bread currently used at Calvary is a type of pita bread, except in Lent when a home-baked bread is provided by volunteering parishioners. The Altar Guild quickly realized that the traditional ciborium, a good fit for holding wafers, was too small for the new type of bread. Two members went in search of a container of some sort into which the new bread would fit. While in a local antique shop one day, one member steadied her stance by placing her hand on a shelf. The other member looked at the shelf, and noticed an extremely tarnished silver wire bowl. The two immediately recognized possibilities. The bowl was purchased, cleaned, and now is used at most Eucharists. Early in the 21st century, Calvary began offering gluten-free wafers that are kept in a small lidded wooden cup.

Current Duties for (Male and Female) Members of the Altar Guild

Flowers are placed on the reredos shelf each Sunday except during Lent and when the Eucharist is celebrated in the Oasis courtyard in summer. The Flower Person is responsible for contacting individuals who wish to donate flowers, determining a date for their display and contacting a florist for arranging flowers in Calvary's vases for delivery on Friday.

In 2008, the Guild treasurer's duties simplified. The accounting and paying of bills was assumed by the Calvary office, although the Guild maintains control over expenditures from its account.

The positions of sub-directress and directress were renamed after the induction of several gentlemen into the Guild. The sub-director is now responsible for ordering supplies. The director is tasked with scheduling workers for all services including weddings and funerals and for monthly cleaning, as well as the overall functioning of the Guild. This position also sees to the replacement of worn linens and repairs of any damaged items.

Vessels and Linens: Yesterday and Today

Over the years, Calvary's Altar Guild has been very fortunate in its financial resources. Donations through the designated envelopes in the pledge-envelope box generally provide enough income to cover expenses for wine, bread, and cleaning fees. The Guild also has been fortunate to have several generous donations, which provide for the purchase of vestments and acolyte robes, and the replacement of worn items. Each item for liturgical celebration has a special use.

Vessels

At Calvary there are precious silver pieces: cruets (small pitchers), a flagon (a large pitcher), a finger bowl; baptismal bowl and shell; a bread basket; and several ciboriums and patens, used to hold the wafers. There are also a cruet and a flagon of crystal. The aumbry, maintained by the Guild, stores reserve elements for the Eucharist taken to shut-ins; the sanctuary candle burns over the aumbry to indicate the presence of these elements. The original silver and crystal pieces for use at the Eucharist have worn out and been replaced. Calvary's oldest silver piece is a refurbished late-19th century silver chalice with a large embossed knop (a decorated knob).

Many of the silver, brass, and crystal pieces have been donated as memorials. Examples include a silver chalice, paten and ciborium set; a pair of matching chalices; alms basins; candle extinguishers; processional crosses; brass vases; and the brass cover for the Gospel book. These and other items are generally purchased from church supply houses.

Linens

In addition to the fair linen protecting the altar, other linens include:

- credence cloths for the small table by the altar and the shelf on the nave in the back where the elements are kept

- purificators, used to wipe the chalice
- a towel (used with a bowl) for drying the rector's hands before Communion

- the corporal, which the rector or deacon spreads on the altar and on which the elements are placed

- a pall of stiffened linen to cover the chalice

- a special towel used at baptisms

- miniature purificators that are placed in the "traveling communion boxes" to enable the rector or deacon to take the Eucharist to those who are unable to attend services at Calvary.

Hangings and Vestments

The hangings are the beautiful cloth pieces that adorn the pulpit and lectern and cover the chalice, as well as the frontal that hangs from the front of the altar. None of the original hand-made hangings and linens survives, but Guild members still launder and iron the replacements.

Today, Calvary is fortunate to have a set of hangings of appropriate color for each season of the church year, as it does for the rector's and deacon's vestments. Vestments, the garments worn by those who serve at the altar, may include the alb, amice, cassock, cincture (girdle), cotta, chasuble, cope, stole, and surplice. In the current world of working women and very busy lives, these items are now purchased and laundered professionally.

The St. Margaret's Altar Guild of Calvary may no longer require attendance at monthly meetings, given busy work schedules. Its members may include men as well as women, listed now by first and last names. We may not wear capes and caps, nor launder and iron the vestments by hand, but our purpose in serving the Lord continues as it has since the founding of the Church—our many members taking care in their tasks and finding great reward and fellowship in them.

ADENDUM

Lenten Bread, Double Recipe

7/8 cup or more lukewarm water

1 packet dry yeast

6 Tbs. honey

3 Tbs. olive oil

½ tsp. salt

5 and 1/3 cups whole wheat flour

Add yeast to water, stirring until yeast dissolves. Add dissolved yeast to honey, oil, salt and unsifted flour in a large mixing bowl. Mix thoroughly by hand. If the flour does not dampen completely, add more water by tablespoon until it is damp. Turn dough out onto a very lightly floured board. Knead for about five minutes until the dough is nice and elastic. Place the dough back in the bowl, cover with a damp cloth and let rise for an hour to an hour and a half in a warm place until it has doubled in bulk. Turn it out onto a lightly floured board and knead for a moment. Roll out to a quarter inch thickness and cut into round loafs of appropriate size (see below). Make a cross by pressing a blade of a knife part way through each loaf so it can be divided into quarters. Transfer to a lightly oiled baking sheet and bake in a 350 degree oven for 10 to 12 minutes. The loaves may be sealed in plastic bags and frozen for future use.

2 inch loaf makes about 12 communions

Campbell's soup can size makes about 25 communions

Tuna fish can size makes about 50 communions

Photo by Penny Duffy

Choir camp, 1916. From a scrapbook kept by lifetime Calvary member Ernest Schlitgus (1901-1982).

Chapter 8

Music and Choral Arts

By Brian A. Williams

Before Calvary had a church building, and almost as soon as it had a rector, there was music. From 1860 to 1863, while the congregation awaited completion of its building, services were held in various locations. The rector, the Rev. Charles W. Woodward, carted a hand-held organ or "melodeon" to each location to accompany the hymns.

Calvary isn't unique in its long-standing commitment to music. You'll find the same story in other Episcopal church histories. Music has always served as a means of inspiration, celebration, focus, and meditation in Episcopal worship. Hymn singing by the congregation, as well as by choirs, is embedded in the Episcopal tradition.

We don't know what hymns were sung at Calvary in those early years. Time and humidity have robbed us of the sheets of music—they rotted away in the old choir room, which has since been described as a "humidity zone." We can only assume that the music followed the styles of the day. Luckier than many parishes, we had the means to secure very competent musicians from early on, and, thankfully, high quality has always been the driving force.

Perhaps with that in mind, not long after Calvary's founding, the parish replaced the melodeon. In August 1864, the women's Sewing Society

The St. Cecilia window

Photo by Amanda Duhrman

bought a Mason & Hamlin cabinet organ with a carved and paneled black walnut case. We don't know who played the organ before 1867, but in that year, the records list a Miss Whalen as organist and Mrs. Torris Cowles as choir director. The choir was made up entirely of volunteers.

As the parish worked to establish itself, there was a fairly high turnover of organists. Of note, Mrs. Emma F. Judd served as both organist and choir director from 1871 to 1875. The stained-glass window near the present organ, depicting St. Cecilia, patron saint of music, was given in her memory by her sons, Dr. E. Starr Judd and C.M. Judd, in 1905.

Like so much else at Calvary, the parish's music rose to a new level during the rectorship of the Rev. William W. Fowler. Shortly after arriving in 1889, he organized Calvary's first vested boys' choir. Louise Mayo, wife of the first Dr. Mayo, supplied materials and sewed cottas and cassocks for the new choristers. For the next thirty years, Calvary had a men and boys' choir, as was preferred at that time.

In another common practice, local newspapers used to report on worship services. In 1891, for example, Calvary's Thanksgiving services were described in the *Olmsted County Democrat*:

> *At Calvary Church on Thursday the anthem which takes the place*
> *of the Venite was sung and Master Bunn Willson of the surplice choir*
> *sang a solo. The sermon by Rev. W.W. Fowler was founded on the anthem*
> *for the day entitled "Praises of Jehovah."*

A Hired Hand to Pump the Pipe Organ

Calvary was fortunate to obtain a W. W. Kimball pipe organ fairly early on. Installed in 1904, it had to have air manually pumped into its chamber. According to the 1960 parish history, the human " 'pumper' had to work hard to keep the 'air gauge' at the proper level, and the organist had to remember not to play the 'full' organ too long, as the wind occasionally would give out, with disastrous results to the music." The history goes on to note that the vestry hired a man to perform this service, but that on occasion volunteers had to fill in. George Melcher, who later collaborated on the design of the massive bronze doors of the Mayo Clinic's Plummer Building, was one of them. We can assume there was a sigh of relief when an electric blower was installed in 1917.

Boys' Choirs and Camps

By 1905, the year after the pipe organ's installation, the choir had grown to 31 members. Mr. Fowler apparently was adept at discerning good voices in the congregation and equally adept at encouraging parents to send their sons to choir practice.

Shortly after the Rev. Arthur H. Wurtele arrived in 1912, the parish engaged a new organist and choirmaster, Harry R. Lucey. The boys sang at both the 10:30 a.m. and Sunday evening services year round, and rehearsed after school every Monday, with a second rehearsal including adults on Thursday.

A Sunday afternoon choir hike, 1913.
From Ernest Schlitgus' scrapbook.

According to the 1960 parish history, Mr. Lucey "had served an apprenticeship in the Merchant Marines and was inclined toward athletics." He took the boys on Sunday afternoon hikes to what was called, with a storybook flourish, "Horsethief Caves," located in the area of the Rochester Community and Technical College, not far from Quarry Hill Park and what was once the Rochester State Hospital. These adventures were followed by chocolate and cakes, consumed in the State Hospital suite of Dr. A.F. Kilbourne, a vestry member and Sunday School teacher at Calvary and supervisor of the hospital.

Back in the 1890s, the boys' choir had begun holding a week-long choir camp every summer at Lake Shady in Oronoco. When Rev. Wurtele and Mr. Lucey were in charge in the early 20th century, the camp moved to Clear Lake in Waseca.

Choir Direction and Expansion: World War I through the Baby Boom

In 1915, after Mr. Lucey moved to St. Paul, Calvary hired an English-born choirmaster, John Leopold Fenwick. Mr. Fenwick had an international background, having studied voice and piano in Germany and trained under Sir John Stainer, an organist and composer of church music in England. Under Mr. Fenwick's leadership, the choir grew to fifty members. It became known as "The Rochester Knight Choristers of Calvary Episcopal Church" and began giving local concerts. Rehearsals increased to two afternoons each week for the boys, plus an all-choir rehearsal on Thursday evening. Choir camp was held at Lake Pepin near Lake City, with residents of the surrounding area coming to hear the concert-by-the lake that the choir gave before breaking camp. Mr.

Fenwick left Calvary in 1917 and moved to Lake City (his son, the Rev. Robert Fenwick, later served as associate rector at Calvary and as the first rector at St. Luke's).

At that time Calvary was blessed with the architectural skills of Harold Crawford, who designed Brackenridge Hall and other parts of the church as well as many of the "Pill Hill" homes in Rochester. His wife, May, had studied opera in Berlin. She directed Calvary's choir from 1919 to 1921 and continued to sing soprano for decades afterwards.

The boys' choir with Rev. Wurtele, 1924

By the early 1920s, the number of boys in the choir had dwindled, and women were allowed back in. Calvary's longest-serving choir director, Mrs. Lillian Trost, had between twenty and thirty choir members at any one time during her tenure from 1921 to 1945. She had to buy new music because most of the music in the church library was written primarily for boys' voices. During this time, in 1933, Calvary replaced the original 1904 organ with a new Kimball pipe organ.

Mrs. Trost was succeeded by Miss Hazel Martin, one of Calvary's most beloved choir directors. A graduate of the Oberlin Conservatory of Music and recipient of two diplomas from the French Conservatory in Fontainebleau, Miss Martin had served briefly as organist under Mr. Fenwick from 1915 to 1917. After returning to Calvary in 1934, she served as organist under Mrs. Trost, becoming choir director in 1945. She continued and expanded the children's choir program during the post-war baby boom until her retirement in 1956. It's hard to imagine, but at one time, 58 children were in that choir. One can only wonder where they put them all!

Gerald Near

Liturgical and Hymnal Changes: Staying on the Cutting Edge

Amid the well-known social upheavals of the 1960s and '70s, another revolution was taking place in the Episcopal church. Calvary was fortunate, once again, to have a superb musician to guide the parish through these changes. When Gerald Near became organist and choirmaster in 1969, planning was already underway for the 1982 Hymnal and the revised 1979 Book of Common Prayer, which included substantial changes in the liturgy. Gerald, who went on to gain international fame as a composer, was proactive in preparing Calvary for what lay ahead. Experimental liturgies, which evolved into Rite II, were already being published, and Gerald introduced them at Calvary. He also started writing music to go with these experimental liturgies. We were, thus, on the cutting edge.

We tend to associate Prayer Book revisions with a modernizing of language, but much of the 1979 alterations involved a return to more ancient practices. There, too, Gerald was in the forefront. At Calvary he reintroduced the office of Evensong, sung once a month, and the Great Vigil of Easter.

Many of Gerald's organ and choral works were written while he was at Calvary. Calvary provided him the freedom to write and present new music. Calvary also provided him with a benefactor in the person of Elizabeth G. Lowry. Calvary's current pipe organ, dedicated in 1974, was a gift from Mrs. Lowry in memory of her mother, Blanche Brackenridge Graham. Blanche Graham was Margaret Brackenridge's daughter, and at one time served as Calvary's organist. Mrs. Lowry is memorialized in one of Gerald's hymns, which is named "Lowry." It is Hymn No. 454, "Jesus came, adored by angels," in the 1982 Hymnal.

Although Gerald was no longer at Calvary when the organ was dedicated, he was the driving force behind its installation. He was not satisfied with the old Kimball organ, which is now in Emmanuel Episcopal Church in Rushford. It's a lovely organ, but was designed more for choral accompaniment than strong hymn leadership. Also, in the early 1970s, tastes favored more "sparkle" and less "gravity" in the organ's sound. Gerald determined that, for the new Hymnal that was coming and for the vast organ literature that was then available, a new organ was needed.

Elizabeth Lowry

He approached Robert Noehren, chair of the organ department at the University of Michigan, where Gerald had studied. Noehren resisted the task. Calvary was too small, he said, and the organ would be located in a "closet" near the altar and would have to "scream its way down the room." Gerald, I'm told, had to beg him to do this project. Noehren once told me that in designing Calvary's organ, he was asked to do the impossible—and he did! The organ was actually built by David Harris of Whittier, California, to Noehren's specifications. It is the only instrument on which Harris and Noehren collaborated (see Chapter 14 for more on the Noehren-Harris organ).

Shortly after the organ's dedication in April 1974, Larry Reynolds became Calvary's music director. He, too, helped Calvary stay on the cutting edge. Like Gerald, he made great use of the new liturgical resources as soon as they became available and was trying new things even before the 1979 Book of Common Prayer was officially published. He also composed Psalms, descants, and an anthem—"Sweet was the song the Virgin sung"—published by Gerald Near's publishing house.

Larry founded the St. Cecilia Choir School in the fall of 1979, and it grew rapidly. It met once a week after school, and the sessions included crafts and a meal as well as voice training and choir rehearsal. The choir participated regularly in Calvary's 9:00 a.m. service and in the diocese's annual Choir Festival at St. Mark's Cathedral in Minneapolis. During Larry's tenure Dr. Mark Lowry, Elizabeth Lowry's husband, purchased a set of Orff (small percussion) instruments for the children's choirs.

Ray and Mary Gustafson served as organist and choirmasters for ten years, from 1987 to 1997. Among their varied contributions to the music program were the continuation of the children's choir and the reorganization of the parish choir into the Motet Choir, a configuration which continues to this day. They purchased the robes that are still worn by the choir, and in 1989 they saw the completion of improvements to the organ. In addition, they formed and directed a parish Folk Choir.

Calvary's Music in the 21st Century

Although Calvary is not unique in its commitment to music, it certainly has a unique heritage on which to build. The congregation is musically talented and inclined to participate. When I arrived in 1998, I assumed that during the Psalm, the congregation wanted to sing only the antiphons and let the choir chant the verses. I was quickly informed that, no, the congregation was used to chanting the verses, and liked it that way. My

Psalm settings quickly changed to reflect that tradition.

The parish's primary approach to music is "good taste, good taste, good taste." We forbid pre-recorded music and stick to the motto, "if you want it, you do it." It's a simple philosophy: nothing fake enters that room. We don't do fake theology, fake religion, fake music or fake anything else. Whatever it is, it's real.

But "traditional" does not mean "unvaried." One of the wonderful things about the Episcopal hymnal is that the hymns are not just Anglican but come from other traditions, including Lutheran, Gregorian chant, Shape-Note/Southern Harmony, Moravian, and Reformed/Presbyterian. At Calvary we also have begun using more hymns from supplemental hymnals such as *Voices Found*, which has hymns with lovely texts written by women. Our worship often draws on original compositions by Calvary's various music directors.

Choirs

We are extremely fortunate to have such dedicated choirs, including the Motet Choir of youth and adults. Both the general choristers and soloists perform magnificently every Sunday and on high holidays. We also have excellent musicians who play woodwinds, bells, and other instruments at the occasional service.

Calvary's long tradition of children's choir continues into the 21st century. The choir is vested, and the children are worship leaders. They don't just stand there singing little songs separate from the service; they are part of the service itself. The first task at rehearsal is practicing the upcoming hymns and Psalm, and the children serve as cantors. They all want to do it—at rehearsal they shout, "My turn! My turn!" "I've never done it!" "She did it last week!" Oh, the mayhem that ensues! It's just

THE CALVARY CHOIRS IN 2009

Motet Choir –
approximately 22 members, adults and youth

Canterbury Choir –
4 members, grades 7-9

St. Cecilia Choir –
7 members, grades 3-6

St. Nicholas Choir –
4 members, grades K-2

Handbell Choir –
9 members, intergenerational

wonderful! In addition to healthy singing techniques, the children learn basic liturgy so they know what they're doing in the service, what season we are in, where it fits in the liturgical year, and what is unique about each season and feast day.

Calvary's Music in the Community

The children's choir participates in the annual Episcopal Youth Music Festival in Minneapolis, and both the adult and children's choirs occasionally sing at other churches. It is one way for Calvary to maintain connections to the diocese, our sister parishes, and the community. A series of weekly organ recitals, started by Jeffrey Daehn in 1997 when he was interim music director, is held during Advent. We also occasionally host other organ and instrument recitals in the church; it's a nice room for small groups and individual instruments—all the wood in that room warms up the sound.

Photo by Cara Edwards

The St. Cecilia choir with Brian Williams, 2009.

Calvary lacks space to do "big orchestra" pieces, and brass buries the choir in that room. We have, however, presented beautiful pieces with ensembles. For example, when we did *The Messiah* in 2002, we had a string quartet, string bass, harpsichord, and two oboes. For the Fauré *Requiem* in 2004, we had string quartet plus string bass, timpani, and two French horns.

Knocking the Dust out of the Pipe Organ

One of Calvary's major efforts in recent years has been looking after the Noehren-Harris organ. There was a design flaw in the winding system which was repaired in 2000. The organ was rewired in 1989 and probably cleaned, at least superficially, at that time. But in the intervening years, during the installation of sprinklers and insulation in the attic which involved workmen walking over the organ's ceiling, dust and debris coated the insides of the pipes. The reed pipes were especially dirty. In addition to cleaning the pipes, the organ chambers were repainted with acrylic paint which helps to focus the sound outward; the chambers had originally been painted with latex, which absorbs sound. The ceiling of one of the chambers was also repaired, because the plaster was giving way and was about to fall onto the pipes.

Jeff Daehn, who is carillonneur for the Mayo Clinic as well as the curator of the Calvary organ and most of the other pipe organs in this part of Minnesota, has been absolutely essential in carrying out this maintenance. The difference in sound is incredible. As Jeff says, it's "snappier" now. And so it is.

A Sweet Liturgical Rhythm

Perhaps the most important musical tradition maintained at Calvary is the accompaniment for the special services that so enrich liturgical life. On the first Sunday of Advent, the parish does either a Service of Lessons and Carols or the "O" Antiphons. Each of the three Christmas Eve services is preceded by a half hour of special music. Transfiguration Sunday generally includes a special anthem or solo, to punctuate the end of the season of Epiphany.

Lent brings as much or more music as any other season—it's just different. The pipe organ is subdued—no high pitches, no big reeds.

LITURGY AT CALVARY

Until 1999 Calvary used Rite I at two services (8:00 and 11:00). The Motet Choir sang at 11:00, and the children's choirs led Rite II worship at 9:00. A newly formed Worship Committee decided to use Rite II at 11:00 except during Lent, when Rite I would be used. In addition, under the leadership of Brian Williams, the choirs began "swapping" services once a month, with the children singing at 11:00 and the adults singing at 9:00. Calvary's website lists the choirs and their anthems, as well as the Organ Voluntary and Postlude, for every service.

Psalms are chanted and anthems sung without accompaniment more often than in other seasons. The emphasis is on the voices of the people rather than the organ. As a result, the services are quiet and meditative. It's a nice change—for six weeks …

Holy Week is, of course, the most significant (and musically grueling!) week of the year. We do Tenebrae on Wednesday and Holy Eucharist on Maundy Thursday. Saturday evening brings the Great Vigil of Easter, when we sing the Exultet and then, once the resurrection is proclaimed, the stops are literally pulled out on the organ. All three services on Easter morning are full choral Eucharists and the two later services feature brass quintet, timpani, and cymbals. Other major feast days, such as Pentecost, Holy Cross Day (Calvary's titular feast) and All Saints, also call for enhanced music.

It is a sweet liturgical rhythm. Calvary is blessed with musicians who willingly share their voices and instrumental talents, thus enriching our worship. We are blessed as well with a long history of dedication and support for the musical and choral arts. As it always has been at Calvary and throughout the Episcopal Church, our goal continues to be to glorify God and enhance the congregation's worship.

A D D E N D U M

Calvary's Musical Instruments

Pianos

We are fortunate to have two lovely Steinway grand pianos. The Brackenridge Hall piano was owned by Hazel Martin and probably was purchased by her in 1923. She bequeathed it to Calvary when she died in 1959. It was rebuilt and refinished locally in 1999. The choir-room Steinway dates from 1906 and was owned by May Crawford. It was part of the Crawford estate that Calvary inherited upon Harold's death in 1981. That piano was rebuilt by a technician in Indianapolis in 1992.

An old friend is about to make its way back to Calvary in the form of a very large, ornately carved George Steck upright piano from 1890. It was perhaps originally purchased for Calvary's old Guild Hall and then was moved to the children's chapel. Having spent a good part of the last century in a house in Oronoco, it is about to return to Calvary, and when it does, its very size and string length may just give the Steinway grands a run for their money!

Harpsichord

The harpsichord was a valuable find. We can thank Jeff Daehn for this one—he was tuning at Luther College in Decorah, Iowa, when he heard about a harpsichord for sale. It was built by Jones-Clayton of Los Angeles in the late 1960s and eventually purchased by Luther College. The college's full-time piano technician, Conrad Hoffsummer, completely rebuilt the instrument in 1989 so that it now functions much like an authentic Baroque harpsichord. We bought it from Luther College for $2,500. Patti Merrill, who sang soprano in the Motet Choir, gave it to Calvary in memory of her mother, Pauline Pool. The estimated cost for a comparable new instrument would be around $30,000.

Bells and Percussion

Calvary has a three-octave set of Schulmerich handbells, a three-octave set of Schulmerich hand chimes, full set of Orff instruments (percussion for children), and a pair of timpani.

Adopted June 1860 By the ladies of Calvary Church —

Constitution of the Sewing Society of Calvary Church Rochester, Minnesota

Art 1st This Society shall be called the *Parish Aid* ~~Sewing~~ Society of Calvary Church Rochester.

Art 2nd The design of this Society is, to aid the cause of Benevolence and that of Religion in the Protestant Episcopal Church. The particular objects to be determined on, at the time, by a vote of the Society.

Art 3 The officers shall be a President, Vice-President, Treasurer and Secretary—all to be elected by ballot, their terms of office to be one year. The annual meeting for the election of officers shall take place on the *Easter Monday at 10 o'clock* ~~first regular meeting after Easter Monday of each year~~. At this meeting the Secretary and Treasurer shall make their report for the last year. The Society shall also meet together

The original records of the Sewing Society. This first entry is dated June 14, 1860.

Chapter 9

Calvary's Churchwomen: Where Would We Be without the Women?

By Jan Larson and Barbara Toman

Exactly one week after Calvary's founding, the women had organized. Meeting on June 14, 1860, at the home of Henrietta Head, wife of vestryman George Head, fifteen women formed "The Sewing Society of Calvary Church." The constitution stated that "The design of this society is to aid the cause of Benevolence and Religion in the Protestant Episcopal Church." Charlotte Woodward, wife of the rector, was the first president. Margaret Brackenridge and Serena Blakely were the other officers.

The ladies set out at once to earn money and have been doing so ever since. They sewed and knitted stockings, nightcaps, aprons, shirts, mittens and hoods, selling them for $1 a piece. They had a booth at the state fair, which was then sometimes held in Rochester. They conducted an annual Christmas market at the German Library Hall at 19 South Broadway. By 1870, the group was called "The Ladies Parish Aid Society"; according to parish records, that was the year they paid to replace the chancel window. Later, they were credited with paying for a new chimney and an "elegant" carpet in

Henrietta Head

Charlotte Woodward

117

the church. For a number of years, this group apparently paid the interest on the church mortgage.

An Ice Cream Parlor in the Post Office

The oldest item in Calvary's archives is a notebook containing the original minutes and accounts of the Sewing Society. The first entry, penned in beautiful, slanting script, lists six articles of organization "Adopted June 1860 By the ladies of Calvary Church." A seventh article, written sideways in the margin, reads: "It shall be the duty of any Lady having agreed to entertain the society upon failure thereof to find a substitute, and report the same to the President."

For the early churchwomen, raising money was essential to fund charitable work and to build the new parish. Fundraising wasn't their only purpose, of course. Fellowship has always been a big part of their mission. In the decades before women were ordained or permitted to serve on vestries, the various churchwomen's organizations allowed women to be involved in important aspects of Calvary's parish life.

They must have had fun doing so. In 1885, the churchwomen operated an ice cream parlor in the basement of the old Post Office, raising enough money to build Calvary's first rectory that same year. When the women decided the parish needed a Guild Hall, to accommodate the Sunday School and the Ladies' Parish Aid meetings, they provided funds for one to be built in 1891. A choir concert was sponsored to help pay for the construction. In 1900, the ladies of Calvary parish staged an amateur production called "The Old Maids' Convention" at the Grand Opera House, at the northwest corner of Broadway and Second Street SW. That effort netted $100, which was used to build a 20-by-10 foot kitchen addition to the Guild Hall.

Changing Names, Continuous Service

If you're not familiar with Calvary, the names of the women's groups over the years can be a little confusing. In the early 20th century, the

Ladies' Parish Aid apparently was divided into several small sewing societies, each of which worked on its own projects. These societies were called by the names of the women who headed them. Two other women's groups also existed at this time: St. Margaret's Guild, which began in 1912 as part of a youth group, but later was comprised of young women; and the Woman's Auxiliary. Although the membership of the latter was practically identical with that of the Ladies' Parish Aid, it was a separate organization with its own officers and treasury. The Auxiliary functioned chiefly during Lent, when members served luncheons and did missionary sewing. A study program often followed.

Margaret Brackenridge

Paying for Salaries, Vestments, Youth, and Street Paving

As Calvary grew in the early 1900s, the churchwomen funded more endeavors. Church suppers were held frequently and were extremely profitable. The first rummage sale took place in 1906; these sales became so popular that the women often held six a year. By then, the Ladies' Parish Aid was paying the choirmaster's and sexton's salaries, the fuel and light bill for church and rectory, and the taxes and insurance on the church property, in addition to making substantial yearly payments on the church debt. In 1907, the Ladies' Parish Aid paid the city of Rochester $373.95 for street paving and curbing.

When Calvary's choir began growing in the 1910s, the churchwomen devoted many meetings to making or repairing choir vestments. In 1920, the ladies decided to pay the vestry $50 a month to help with choir expenses. This pledge remained in effect until 1939, when the Ladies' Parish Aid assumed full responsibility for the choir and organist, pledging $750 and later $1,000 per year for that purpose. The commitment lasted for decades. When the Sunday School choir was organized in 1951, the Parish Aid provided the money to have vestments made for the children.

Calvary's youth were also funded by the churchwomen. The Ladies' Parish Aid gave financial assistance to the Boy Scout and Girl Scout troops sponsored by Calvary in the 1920s. For six years, the women also helped the Young People's Fellowship (YPF), an Episcopal youth group, put on an annual Christmas party for about forty underprivileged children. Whenever YPF conventions were held in Rochester, the women served the meals and arranged for housing for the visitors.

Cooking and Sewing to the Benefit of All

Sewing always seemed to be a part of the Ladies' Parish Aid meetings. Many a comforter was tied, towels and tablecloths hemmed, and aprons made. Special sewing projects were undertaken, such as making layettes for the community-health nurse and sewing for the Red Cross during the wars. During the Depression, from 1931 to 1933, a sewing class was conducted in the basement of Brackenridge Hall to help needy women make their own clothes. Materials were furnished by the Parish Aid, and the instruction was given by Aid members.

Of course, the ladies also did a lot of cooking. The numbers are staggering. On November 25, 1935, at Calvary's diamond jubilee celebration, the Ladies' Parish Aid served a turkey dinner to 225 people at a cost of 35 cents per plate. Parish records note several other large receptions over the next thirty years or so, given in honor of incoming or retiring clergy.

The women reorganized a little in the 1930s. By 1933, the Woman's Auxiliary and Ladies' Parish Aid held joint meetings. The Parish Aid was divided into three groups, known as A, B, and C. In 1937, St. Margaret's Guild joined the Aid, making a fourth group. Then, of course, in 1939 the fruitcake project began (see Chapter 12).

U.S.O. Parties in Brackenridge

For eighteen months during World War II, the churchwomen gave up their personal use of Brackenridge Hall and furnished it as a reading and recreation room for the Air Force men who were training at Rochester airport as a glider unit. U.S.O. parties were held in Brackenridge Hall, and a number of Calvary Church women assisted with the entertainment.

In 1943, Blanche Graham established a fund of $5,000, with the interest to be used by the Ladies' Parish Aid to maintain Brackenridge Hall. (In 1917, she and her husband, Dr. Christopher Graham, had donated the Hall, which is named after her mother, Margaret Brackenridge). Calvary's churchwomen also funded a snack bar, complete with china and glassware, at the Merry-Go-Round, a YWCA recreation center established in 1945.

Blanche Graham

A Centennial Tableau. Calvary Episcopal Churchwomen recreate earlier times as part of the parish's 1960 celebration.

Candy for "forgotten patients." Each Christmas in the 1960s, Calvary's churchwomen wrapped packages of candy for patients at the State Hospital in Rochester.

Reorganizing into the CEC

After World War II, as Calvary's membership ballooned, the churchwomen's membership was broadened and simplified. In 1948, the Ladies' Parish Aid and Woman's Auxiliary officially became one organization, patterned after the diocesan and national woman's auxiliaries. Every woman of Calvary Church now automatically became a member of the Woman's Auxiliary Guild, which functioned as a part of the diocesan organization as well as on the local level. Groups A, B, and C dissolved, and the active membership was divided into seven groups or guilds, one of which was St. Margaret's Guild. Several of the new groups named themselves for women who had been active in the church in previous years, such as the Mary Graham Group, the Gertrude Berkman Group, and the Helen Judd Group. At this time Calvary also had several small groups of younger women who met at their various homes in the evening to socialize and work on projects.

Collectively, they were called the Junior Aid. Most of these young women eventually joined the larger groups.

All of these women's groups continued to fund major expenses. In 1954, the Woman's Auxiliary Guild donated $200 to help the vestry meet the assessment required of our parish for the Anglican Congress held in Minneapolis. In 1955, the Guild gave $675 to the vestry toward the debt incurred by the purchase of the new rectory. The women also contributed to the fund to send the Rev. O. Wendell McGinnis, Calvary's rector, and his wife, Charlotte, to the General Convention in Hawaii.

By 1960—a century after the founding of the Sewing Society of Calvary Church—the notion of being extra and subsidiary no longer seemed to describe the churchwomen's work. In response to a suggestion from the national organization that the word "auxiliary" be dropped, Calvary changed the group's name to Calvary Episcopal Churchwomen. Calvary's rector, the Rev. Sam Cook, subsequently suggested that the guilds be disbanded and the churchwomen operate as a single organization. The "CEC," as it was known, continued to raise money from rummage sales, an annual bazaar, and the fruitcake project. It also ran a parish bridge marathon.

Under the CEC steering committee, the fundraising and social work continued into the 21st century. The women bought furnishings for the church and planned and carried out social functions. By 1985, the CEC's annual pledge to the church had grown to $4,000. During the Oasis Building project, the CEC paid for the large Crawford cross on the west side of the building, as well as for one of the panes in the new healing window. Besides fruitcake, the largest fundraisers—and social events— were the annual rummage sale in spring, and the fall bazaar.

"FIRSTS" FOR WOMEN AT CALVARY

In 1986, Jan Larson was elected Calvary's first female senior warden. Jan was responsible for calling the Rev. Nicklas Mezacapa to be Calvary's rector that same year. Six years later, in 1992, the Rev. Ginny Padzieski became Calvary's first female deacon.

The bazaar was the highlight of the fall season, and many people participated in getting ready for it. The fruitcake was already baked and ready to sell; other baked goods, hangers, cutlery, crafts, attic treasures, and a delicious luncheon were all featured. Chaired by Sally Duffy, the luncheon became so popular that several seatings were needed. Marie Doty and Beanie Kettlehut kept the hobby hut crafts available year round; Eleanor Kirklin and Evie Devine knitted Christmas socks, which always had a waiting list to be purchased. The Johnsons spent several days getting ready for "Attic Treasures," which was greatly anticipated by the general public.

Photo by Ian Jarman

CEC bazaar in 2002. Kay Eppard and Margaret Sinclair staff the fruitcake table.

The Churchwomen's Legacy—From Sewing Society to Parish Committees

Little by little, the number of CEC participants began to decline due to age, ill health, and death. By the 1990s younger women, who increasingly worked outside the home, did not have time to participate. The decision in the early 21st century to disband the bazaar was difficult, but necessary due to lack of helping hands. The rummage sale was resurrected by the youth mission-trip group in 2006.

As the years went on, other groups at church took over the social responsibilities previously assumed by the churchwomen. By the late 1990s, Calvary had a fellowship committee that planned special parties and events as well as a corps of Sunday morning coffee hosts. A building and grounds committee looked after church maintenance and furnishings.

The churchwomen's original Sewing Society was, thus, the ancestor of almost every group or committee at Calvary. The only task remaining to the churchwomen was the fruitcake baking, which now includes men and youth. That group came to be called "the fruitcake committee," and the CEC largely disbanded.

Of course, the churchwomen are still here, and still working hard to "aid the cause of Benevolence and Religion." But in an era when women serve on vestries and are ordained, and our presiding bishop, the Most Rev. Dr. Katharine Jefferts Schori, is a woman, it perhaps isn't surprising that there is no longer a separate women's organization. Calvary's next parish history may not devote an individual chapter to women. But as we celebrate our 150th year, it would be a grievous error not to remember women's contributions over the years or fail to express our heartfelt gratitude for the blessing of their presence at Calvary.

Where, indeed, would we be without the women?

Dr. Phil Karsell and Frank Hawthorne tour a school in Deschapelles, Haiti, during a Calvary Church mission trip, 2001.

Chapter 10

Christian Social Action

By Frank and Dottie Hawthorne

*"Now go out into the highways and hedges, and look for Jesus in
the ragged and naked, in the oppressed and sweated, in those
who have lost hope, and in those who are struggling to make
good. Look for Jesus in them; and when you find Him, gird
yourselves with His towel of fellowship, and wash His feet in
the person of His brethren."*

---- The Rt. Rev. Frank Weston
Anglican Bishop (1871-1924)

These timeless words confront the faithful—clergy, choristers, and acolytes
among them—who pass through the confines of Calvary's sacristy and look
for Jesus in the sheltered worship space of the sanctuary. Hanging in a frame
next to the sacristy door, Bishop Weston's message has come to symbolize for
many the fundamental Christian challenge facing the larger Calvary family—
a congregation whose "ragged and naked" roots extend from the pioneer
days of the 1850s to the general affluence and optimism of present times.

Calvary has faced that challenge from its beginnings in the frontier village of Rochester. The parish would never have been founded nor the church built without generous outreach by more fortunate, often distant, "others." Having benefited from others' mission zeal, Calvary's parishioners have always sought to give as well. This commitment to humanitarian work has continued in efforts undertaken locally, nationally, and internationally. Through floods of river water and refugees, at a hospital in Haiti and on the sidewalks of Rochester, Calvary searches beyond its own good fortune to give generously, passionately, and personally to meet the needs of the larger world.

Returning the Founders' Generosity

Calvary's founding in 1860 was the result of years of missionary effort extended by the Episcopal Church to "the West," as the Midwest was then known. It was not an easy task. In 1862, when construction began on "Calvary Chapel," Rochester was a booming farm community with a population of about 1,200—large enough to sustain an independent faith community of Episcopalians, but not prosperous enough to build a simple worship space without outside assistance. The first bishop of the Diocese of Minnesota, the Rt. Rev. Henry Benjamin Whipple, offered $500 towards the building of Calvary Church, matched by another $500 gift from his friend, the Rev. Morgan Dix of Trinity Church in New York. The parish itself raised another $500. Donations from back East—including a Bible for the lectern and an engraved communion set—helped furnish the small church.

Once construction of the church was finished in late 1863, the hardy pioneers who comprised the Calvary faith family at last had a home of their own from which to return the founders' generosity. Calvary's first rector, the Rev. Charles Woodward, epitomized the missionary zeal. His labors made possible the growth envisioned by Bishop Whipple. Calvary was not Rev. Woodward's only church. Carrying a small melodeon organ and communion set, he traveled regularly to the communities of Pleasant Grove, Hamilton, High Forest, Chatfield, Oronoco and Mantorville to provide monthly services, and arranged for lay leaders to hold services on intervening Sundays. He often made these journeys on foot, as horses were expensive to maintain, and renting a horse and buggy was a luxury reserved for bad weather or exceptional circumstances. Rev. Woodward was only 45 years old when he resigned as Calvary's rector in 1866, his health having been seriously damaged by the strenuous regime he set himself to grow the church in southeastern Minnesota.

Strong leadership from the congregation also helped Calvary follow the Lord's commandment to "Love your neighbor." Almost as soon as the parish was founded in 1860, women in the congregation organized "The Sewing Society of Calvary Church," later known as the Ladies' Parish Aid Society. Their efforts in the community were not well documented. Might this be because our contemporary notion of "mission" as humanitarian work organized by committee was then part of the very fabric of parish life, too habitual to be noted?

One clue of early outreach work remains. Calvary's parish newsletter from Easter 1938 mentions the Lenten mite boxes in which Church School students collected coins. The newsletter notes: "This offering has been devoted to work among children in various parts of the world since its inception in 1877."

Less than a quarter century after Calvary was founded, the parish faced natural disaster. The devastating tornado of August 1883 struck at a time when Calvary, lacking a rector, was not holding regular services. Nevertheless, Dr. William Worrall Mayo and his sons, Dr. Will and Dr. Charlie (all members of Calvary), tended the injured and dying at various locations in downtown Rochester. The human suffering caused by this tornado led to the fortuitous alliance between the Roman Catholic Sisters of St. Francis and the Episcopalian Drs. Mayo toward the founding of St. Marys Hospital, precursor to the Mayo Medical Center.

As Calvary grew in the 20th century, outreach efforts began to be noted in parish records. "The Young Peoples Guild," a youth group that met for a few months in 1912, raised money for Thanksgiving baskets "for the poor" and eyeglasses "for poor boys." After World War I, the Altar Guild sponsored a French orphan boy. During the Depression, the Ladies' Parish Aid provided materials and held sewing classes in Brackenridge Hall so that needy women could make their own clothes. When an Air Force glider unit began training at Rochester Airport during World War II, Brackenridge Hall was transformed into a reading and recreation room for Service men and a site for U.S.O. parties. After the war, in 1947, Calvary's youth collected twenty boxes of clothing to ship to devastated areas of Europe.

Other, more longstanding efforts were undertaken through outlets provided by the Episcopal Church at the diocesan and national levels. United Thank Offering (U.T.O.) drives—often led by industrious women at Calvary—are annual events to which both adults and children may contribute, secure in the knowledge that their money is being well-utilized. In December 1967, the *Visitor* promised that U.T.O. donations would be responsibly directed to social ministries in North American and Latin American countries, and that even a ministry in nearby Eau Claire, Wisconsin, received a substantial grant of $30,000 from the larger drive.

The Rev. Samuel W. Cook

The 1970s: A New Focus on Outreach

The long tenure of the Rev. Sam Cook as Calvary's rector from 1965 to 1986 was marked by numerous efforts to enhance Calvary's tradition of outreach to the Rochester area community. One was a commitment to having the church worship space stay open 24/7, 365 days a year, for those seeking a place for quiet prayer and meditation.

In addition, in the early 1970s, "Sam," as Rev. Cook was known by his congregation, aided the efforts of the local Church Women United (CWU) chapter to establish a Drop-In Center at Calvary. Mayo Clinic patients arriving in Rochester from near or far often needed directions to find their way around the medical complex, and Rochester itself. Conveniently located, Calvary took the opportunity to offer a comfortable place (the Fireside Room) where the CWU could welcome visitors, offering directions and hotel and restaurant information and a friendly ear to hear visitors' stories. Providing cookies and coffee, CWU maintained the ministry for seventeen years. Marlene McGuire was one of those

The Drop-in Center

Calvary women who put in many hours as a Drop-In Center volunteer. In the late 1980s, the Mayo Clinic constructed a patient cafeteria and vastly improved its patient-information services. These developments, plus an aging corps of CWU volunteers and a dwindling number of visitors seeking directions and advice about accommodations, brought an end to this gentle ministry.

In the late 1970s, Calvary faced a second natural disaster: the "Biblical deluge" of July 5, 1978, when massive rains caused the Zumbro River to crest at 23 feet. The local American Red Cross was so overwhelmed that at least one call for assistance went to its St. Paul chapter. Within hours, five workers were en route to Rochester, among them fellow Episcopalian Mary Hassell. She recommended that Calvary Church, "with its central location and within two blocks of the flooding," should be designated temporary Red Cross Headquarters for the community-relief effort. Rev. Cook, who was himself a Red Cross volunteer, quickly gave his blessing to that open-ended offer.

The Tong Pao family, who arrived from Laos in 1980. Pictured in 1985, from left (from row): Mary Susan, Mai Zia, Mai Lor; (back row) Tong Pao, Mai Xong Lee, Ya Jon.

For the first 48 hours of the crisis, Brackenridge Hall became a sleeping and lunchroom shelter. The legendary Betty Alden organized the churchwomen to make sandwiches and coffee. Another longtime Red Cross volunteer who seemed to be everywhere was Margaret "Peg" Twentyman, whose skills as a professional nurse were utilized. Some women worked round the clock for so long that Mary Hassell recalls having "to send a few home because they were too tired to work. I will always remember what a welcoming community Calvary was when needed."

Calvary's rector was himself in need of aid. Flood waters struck Sam's rectory home on Memorial Parkway. His family, while spared, suffered the loss of many possessions. The church provided generously to the Cooks in their distress and also contributed $2,500 to other parish-family victims.

Another, longer-term project began in the Sam Cook era when refugees from the metastasizing conflicts of Southeast Asia came streaming into southeastern Minnesota in the 1970s. Calvary's refugee-resettlement work continued into the 21st century, when—just before 9/11/2001—a group of young men arrived from Sudan; they were among the so-called "Lost Boys" who had been displaced and/or orphaned by the Sudanese Civil War (1983-2005). Throughout those decades Calvary was quite busy sponsoring a cultural cornucopia of families from not only Asia and Africa, but also Eastern Europe. The Minnesota Council of Church's Resettlement Program directed most of these individuals and family groups to Calvary, but the parish also worked closely with local faith communities and organizations.

Azmeria Gebramlak, who arrived from Ethiopia in 1987.

Some of the newcomers were from equatorial climates and literally walked off their planes at Rochester Airport with no place to call home, little or no English or conversational skills, and without winter coats to face the howling winds of the Minnesota prairie. The Ven. Benjamin Scott, who grew up in the parish, recalls that among the early arrivals were the Hmong, natives of the hill country in Laos. Ben and his wife, Sally, welcomed Hmong families for memorable visits to their farm in Salem Township.

Ben notes, "The Hmong came to us as subsistence farmers from their own simple villages. The women were very talented at handiwork— embroidery on colorful story cloths, and in many creative, time-consuming works. I remember that Peg (Twentyman) and others from

Calvary assisted them in marketing their craftwork in a small shop at the old Zumbro Hotel and in places outside of Rochester." A framed story cloth donated by the Twentyman family hangs just outside Brackenridge Hall as a visual reminder of that outreach work.

Peg Twentyman

Peg and Mary: "Angel Ladies"

Peg Twentyman was one of a pair of extraordinary women at Calvary in the latter 20th century who exemplified how faith-based spirit and hard work can touch lives in the "highways and hedges" far beyond the worship pews. The other was Dr. Mary Goette, who taught at Rochester Community College and was that institution's first female Ph.D. Peg and Mary — sometimes laboring separately, but often in tandem — were friends and fellow toilers in multiple fields of social concern, but especially refugee resettlement. Even though formally allocated parish monies for this cause rarely exceeded $1,000, Peg and Mary spent decades helping dozens of immigrants from diverse countries and cultures settle into new lives in Minnesota.

Mary Goette

One Ethiopian woman, Azemera Behe, now in her 30s and living in Rochester with her two children, recalls meeting the Calvary women as a newly landed, homesick teenager in August 1987. "Peg and Mary were my wonderful angel ladies," she says. "They became like the family I had to leave behind in Africa. They gave me some money to help out each month. They sat with me when I was sick, and generally were just there for me when I needed someone."

Calvary's work with refugees was undertaken in conjunction with other local faith communities. That ecumenical thread has strengthened with Calvary's joining other congregations in various charitable events. One of these, begun in the mid-1980s and still going strong, is the "Crop Walk," an effort by Church World Service and Rochester's Channel One food bank to raise money to feed the hungry both here and abroad. From just a few hundred dollars raised annually in the early years, Calvary has recently recruited multi-generational teams of walkers whose combined pledges exceed $2,000.

Calvary's current rector, the Rev. Nick Mezacapa, known to his parishioners as "Father Nick," often alludes to the fact that "while Calvary is but a small parish in a large community of big churches, we are stronger than our numbers due to our tradition of openness, tolerance, and a heartfelt willingness to work with the greater faith community to help others."

Under Father Nick's guidance, in the 1990s Calvary undertook a reorganization of its finances, in an effort to fund internal projects and external giving. By that time, the booming farm town that was Rochester in 1862 had blossomed into a small city with a prosperous medical and high-tech economy. Calvary has long benefited significantly from the generous gifts of such prominent Rochester families as the Mayos and Harold Crawford, allowing the parish to extend beyond itself. Since at least the 1970s, income from various bequests has provided additional funds for mission and outreach disbursement. From 1978 to 2008, those disbursements totaled more than $325,000, benefiting many local, state, national and global organizations. The committee overseeing such matters has been variously known as Mission & Outreach, Christian Social Action, and, most recently, the Service Core. The latter represents an attempt to refocus parish benevolence on more local social concerns.

But Calvary's engagement with the wider world continues. After a year of fundraising, and with support from the parish, Calvary's "Children of Christ" youth group raised $5,000 for Heifer Project International, a relief group that purchases farm animals for the world's poor. The Calvary project had started in 1999 as an effort to raise $120 to "buy" a goat, but the students insisted on raising funds to buy an "ark," or pair of every kind of animal heifer provides. The Calvary children, who were in grades five through eight at the time, were later honored along with their leader, Nancy Malloy, at the diocesan level with an award from the Sheltering Arms Foundation.

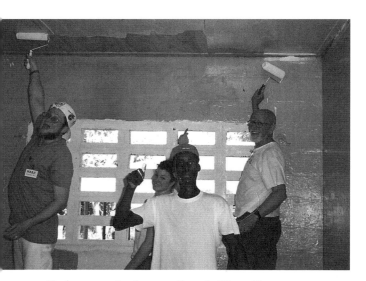

Calvary missioners Frank Hawthorne, Ashleigh Rosson, and Jed Harris help locals paint housing for tuberculosis patients at Hôpital Albert Schweitzer, Deschapelles, Haiti, 2001.

Mission Trips, Near and Far

Apostolic action increased in the 2000s in the form of mission trips in the U.S. and beyond. In 2001, Dr. Phil Karsell—who has spent upwards of a month each year applying his skills as a radiologist for the poorest people in the neediest places around the world—and his wife, Kay, led a trip to the Hôpital Albert Schweitzer in Haiti. There, a team of ten Calvary parishioners spent a week painting houses for tuberculosis patients, perhaps benefiting more from what they learned as Christian "haves" than did the Haitian "have-nots" who received such other gifts as shoes and school supplies. The Calvary folk also had ample opportunities to experience Haiti's spiritual opposites, worshiping in a conventional church setting as well as paying a non-worship visit to the hospitable but voodoo-laden compound of an authentic witch doctor.

The trip to Haiti was so successful that the parish committed to undertaking a youth mission trip every other year. In spring 2004, six high-school students spent a week in New York City, working in a soup kitchen among other efforts. In summer 2006, six students cleared woodland paths and learned about Ojibwe culture at Cass Lake Episcopal Camp. Two years later, thirteen youth and five adults raised $12,000 for a one-week trip to an Episcopal mission in Bay St. Louis, Mississippi, where they helped with cleanup and rebuilding after Hurricane Katrina.

A Downtown Ministry

Although the old Drop-In Center has closed, Calvary continues to strive to minister to people downtown: Mayo Clinic patients and employees, other downtown workers, and parishioners and others who stop by mid-week. Early in his ministry at Calvary, Father Nick conceived the idea of Calvary as an "oasis" downtown: a sanctuary of peace, prayer, and worship, a meeting space, and a garden for outdoor summertime entertainment. One way he achieved this was by mobilizing the parish to turn the rather plain green courtyard, walled in by a massive privet hedge, into an English-style garden "oasis" with flower beds and benches. Every year, on a Sunday morning in mid-May, parishioners gather in gardening clothes to plant thousands of impatiens and other flowering annuals. Most of the hundreds who enjoy this space – including those attending weekly free Oasis Courtyard concerts in the summer – agree that ours is an earthly corner of paradise, at least until the return of seasonal frost and snow and the annual plague of roosting crows.

Within the church's walls, Father Nick and the vestry have continued a long tradition of offering facilities to outside groups needing a weekday place to meet. In recent years these have included such organizations as Alcoholics Anonymous and Narcotics Anonymous. In addition, the church remains open from 8 a.m. to 5 p.m. weekdays for prayer and meditation. Calvary continues to participate in inter-faith connections and activities devoted to issues of diversity in the Rochester community.

Father Nick, Paul Skattum, Sally Arrindell, and Phil Karsell greet passersby at Calvary's Sidewalk Café, 2003.

Father Nick's own reaching out into the community has made him a familiar and popular figure, not to mention a much-in-demand public speaker, to thousands of neighbors who would otherwise not know much about Episcopalians in general or Calvary in particular. Once a month, he takes his ministry "to the street" with an early-morning "Sidewalk Café." He and a handful of parish volunteers stand at the corner of Third Avenue and Second Street SW, simply handing out brief words of encouragement or thematic inspiration (candy, Halloween mask, or some other little remembrance) to pedestrians on their way to work. Those who have experienced any part of Calvary's various faith-in-action adventures over the past 150 years have been as much receivers as givers, truly blessed by the experience and their attempts to "take His towel of fellowship, and wash His feet in the person of His brethren."

140

Chapter 11

Hospital Chaplaincy

By Timothy Hallett

They always called him "Father Brown." I never heard him referred to as anything else, not "Mr. Brown," or "Reverend," or "Chaplain." "Father" was not customary nomenclature among Minnesota Episcopalians of the time. Most would have considered its use an indication of extreme and unseemly Anglo-Catholicism, except in the case of Father Brown. For him it was an expression of affection and respect, just as it should be.

Growing up in Rochester in the 1940s, I had no idea what his first name was, or whether he had a family. Indeed, I did not learn this personal information until I started research for this chapter. His Christian name was George Lewis; he was married and had two children, a son and a daughter. I think he must have been a widower at the time of his retirement in 1946.

Father Brown was the first Episcopal chaplain to the Mayo Clinic hospitals, a ministry that has served tens of thousands of patients of all denominations from around the world and close to home. Offering pastoral services from visitation to sacraments, the chaplaincy has changed in structure over the years but continues its vital ministry to patients in the two Mayo Clinic hospitals.

Father Brown was ideally suited to launch this ministry, having a fairly unusual background for a priest. The Calvary Church archives contain a small scrapbook kept by Father Brown with a few newspaper clippings giving hints of his career. One article, from a Sioux City, Iowa, paper is headlined, "S. C. Ironworker Now Chaplain in Big Mayo Clinic":

> *"Rev. Brown's rise to the ministry is unusual. While employed*
> *as an iron worker in the Novelty Manufacturing company on*
> *Water Street here, he put his nights to use as study periods*
> *under the tutelage of Rev. Robert S. Flockhart. After years of*
> *study, acting as Sunday school instructor and unpaid assistant*
> *to Rev. Flockhart, Rev. Brown was ordained into the Episcopalian*
> *ministry in St. Thomas church in 1926. His first pastorate was at*
> *Charlton in the southern part of Iowa."*

"The Mayo Clinic's Beloved Father Brown"

Father Brown came to Minnesota in November 1928, when he was called to St. Matthew's Church in Chatfield, with charge of Emmanuel Church, Rushford. In December 1931, he was appointed chaplain of the work of the Church at the hospitals connected with the Mayo Clinic, under the sponsorship of the Diocese of Minnesota.   For the time being, he retained the rectorship of St. Matthews, relinquishing the charge at Rushford, and continued to reside in Chatfield. His appointment must have been a tremendous relief to the Rev. Guy Menefee, who had handled the hospital work in addition to his duties as rector of Calvary Church. The extent of the work became immediately apparent. By January 1932, the chaplaincy was made a full-time position. Father Brown and his family moved to Rochester.

Another newspaper clipping in Father Brown's scrapbook, unidentified and undated, notes that the average patient population at the Mayo Clinic hospitals was 2,500, and came from across the U.S. and around the world. Father Brown made anywhere from 600 to 700 visits each month. Besides meeting any emergency calls, he visited each hospital twice a week. "Previous to last February," the article notes, "he ministered primarily to Churchmen and to Eastern Orthodox patients. At that time, however, he was officially asked to visit all patients not cared for by the Roman Catholic, Methodist, and Lutheran chaplains."

In 1944, Father Brown was given the unusual honor of being made a Canon of the Cathedral of Our Merciful Saviour in Faribault. An article from the Faribault paper of June 23 notes that a cathedral chapter confers a canoncy "only for meritorious work" in a chosen field. "Father Brown has served his church well," the article continues. "His work in Rochester has brought him in contact with people from numerous countries and of every social standing. He has worked, walked, and talked with thousands of them. He is the beloved 'Father Brown' of the Mayo Clinic to them and will continue to be so, although his new dignity will entitle him to Canon Brown and to wear ecclesiastical purple."

Father Brown's pastoral load was staggering. In his final report to the Diocesan Convention, he noted that in 1945, 1,746 Episcopalians were registered at Mayo Clinic. In addition, Father Brown said, "the Chaplain was directed to 954 patients who registered no religious affiliation, or a total of 2,700 persons." Some 9,319 calls "were made on Church people; 3,762 on non-denominational or a total of 13,081 calls. The Chaplain had two weddings, twelve burials, and three baptisms. He also had 34 services in different parishes and missions."

The Rev. Leslie Hallett: From Drill Sergeant to Chaplain

Upon Father Brown's retirement in 1946, the Rev. Leslie William Hallett, my father, was appointed chaplain. Like Father Brown, he had read for orders, serving parishes in International Falls, Minnesota, and environs before moving to Fergus Falls as rector of St. James's Church, with charge of churches in the surrounding communities as well. Prior to ordination he had served — improbably to those who knew him later — as a drill sergeant and bayonet instructor in the Canadian Army. After discharge he worked with his father-in-law in the hardware business while studying for ordination.

The Halletts and their large family (with five of seven children still living at home) occupied the spacious, half-timbered house owned by Calvary Church at 311 Third Ave. SW. Father Brown had also lived in the house for some period of his tenure. It was ideally located for the chaplain's residence (for more about life in the rectory, see Chapter 14).

In the summer of 1946, Calvary's newsletter noted that a parish garden party was held "at the homes of Mrs. Henderson and Mrs. Pemberton" to honor Father Brown on his retirement. Drs. Henderson and Pemberton owned neighboring houses on Pill Hill, with adjoining gardens. There is a fine photograph of the occasion, showing Father Brown, Dr. Menefee, and Chaplain Hallett with the hosts. The occasion and the photo speak volumes about the close relation of parish and chaplaincy.

As it had in the time of Father Brown, the Calvary Sunday bulletin listed both the rector and the chaplain, noting that the chaplain was at the service of patients at Mayo Clinic and hospitals. The church was left open 24 hours a day in those much safer times, with the deliberate intention of being available to anyone who felt a need to go there for prayer. My father instituted a service of intercession at noon on weekdays, praying for his long list of patients currently at the Clinic or in the hospitals.

Pill Hill garden party, 1946, honoring Father Brown at his retirement. From left (front row): Dr. Edward Henderson and Dr. John de J. Pemberton; (back row) Rev. Menefee, Father Brown, Chaplain Hallett.

Chaplain Hallett's report for the Diocesan Journal in 1951 counts 1,214 communicants of the Church registered at the Rochester Medical Center, on whom 5,794 calls were made. He also called on 1,128 patients registered as non-denominational, and on those 3,760 calls were made, for a total of 9,554 calls. He conducted 297 weekday services of intercession in the church, had 233 private communions, three baptisms, one wedding, eight burials, 88 other services, and gave four addresses. As I grew older, I often accompanied my father on his Sunday circuit of surrounding communities, sometimes playing the organ or serving as acolyte.

In 1957, the Woman's Auxiliary gave a reception in Brackenridge Hall to celebrate the fortieth wedding anniversary of my parents, Leslie and Rosa Hallett. A television set was presented to them by members of the parish. Ten years later, another reception in the same place celebrated their fiftieth anniversary.

In 1963, my father was awarded an honorary Doctor of Divinity from Seabury-Western Theological Seminary. By then, I was a student at the same seminary, as a postulant from Calvary Church. The parish supported my education with assistance from the Dr. Graham Scholarship Fund. My two older brothers had also followed their father into the priesthood. Like him, both of them completed their careers as hospital chaplains.

"Thanking God that Rev. Hallett Was There"

In 1965, the year of my father's retirement, the diocese and parish arranged a testimonial dinner. Bishop McNairy was chairman of the committee, with Bishop Kellogg as master of ceremonies. Attendees came from as far away as Alaska. Dr. Charles Mayo was among the speakers. There were tributes from colleagues. Both bishops noted that before being elected in Minnesota, they had learned of Chaplain Hallett's grace-filled ministry from many of their parishioners from Texas and New York who had been patients in Rochester. Bishop McNairy remarked, "Only Bishop Kellogg and I know in how many service registers across the Diocese of Minnesota the name of Leslie W. Hallett is written. Everywhere he has been there are those thanking God for the fact that he was there." A flood of letters from former patients confirmed the sentiment.

The Rev. Wesley E. Crowle succeeded Rev. Hallett as chaplain in September 1965, coming to Rochester from Toronto General Hospital. Certification in clinical pastoral education had become the norm for persons engaged in chaplaincy, and he brought those credentials to his ministry. While the Protestant chaplains had always had cordial and collegial relations, closer ecumenical cooperation and more formal structures were increasingly coming into place, and the Roman Catholic Church became a partner in the ecumenical mix. Facilities to assist the ministry of chaplains were provided in the Chaplains' Office of the Methodist Hospital, and space for a chaplains' room was made available at St. Marys Hospital.

As the two hospitals developed separate departments of pastoral care, the Rochester Chaplains' Association began to function as a professional organization. Consultant chaplains organized an on-call system to assure continuous coverage, and the Protestant chaplains took turns conducting Sunday worship in St. Marys Hospital. Chaplains were represented on the executive committee of St. Marys and on the Religious Emphasis Committee at Methodist Hospital. The chaplains' on-call system began to place more emphasis on pre-operative calls the night before surgery as patients increasingly had pre-operative work-ups at the Clinic. Close relation to Calvary Church continued, including the institution of a "Drop-In Center" at Calvary under the auspices of Church Women United, staffed by volunteers from the participating congregations.

Rev. Crowle's reports in the mid-1970s testify to the increasingly ecumenical operation of the chaplaincy, with attendant joys and frustrations. "As I share in the total patient listing in both hospitals, I find that I am seeing as many non-Episcopalians as I do Episcopalians these days. A ministry of the Word and Sacraments is made available to all as we seek to respect denominational preferences … The dream of all working in the health care field is for close mutual cooperation and over the years this is gradually coming about. Progress seems at times slow or non-existent and then may take a spurt forward." At St. Marys, he noted, the Protestant chaplains had been pressing for equal time on the hospital's closed-circuit television and in general "for an opportunity to share on the healing team with a better sense of equality."

Mayo Clinic had no official association with Pastoral Services. Rev. Crowle nevertheless sought closer cooperation between physicians and clerics. *Time* magazine, he noted, "once described the Clinic as the 'Secular Lourdes.' This may point up the need for the representatives of medicine and religion to re-associate more closely for the total care of patients."

When Rev. Crowle wrote his chaplain's report in 1976, the two Rochester hospitals had different patterns for pastoral care. At Methodist the Protestant chaplains were virtually interchangeable among denominations. Like other chaplains, Rev. Crowle served ecumenically as Unit Chaplain for a nursing station. "Some of us however," he added, "function alongside, occasionally within, but generally outside this framework, and see our own denominational patients — myself for one, with of course the R.C. and the more conservative Lutheran groups and some others."

St. Marys was more denominational. Each chaplain ministered to his own faith group, with full-time chaplains and clinical training students also covering patients listed as undesignated Protestant or no-preference. All non-Roman Catholic and Jewish chaplains at St. Marys were supplied by their individual faith communities, making them dependent upon support from their denominations.

Rev. Crowle suggested that a paid Protestant chaplaincy— "an unlikely possibility" at that time—would be needed in future years. "When it is accepted that a trained hospital ministry is what is needed in such a special situation as this one is, one can anticipate how much thinner pastoral care becomes when any denomination withdraws its support as at least one has done in recent years," he said.

The Diocese of Minnesota reaffirmed its commitment to the Episcopal chaplaincy in 1981: "Its purpose is to provide a hospital ministry to Episcopalians from all over the world who come to the Mayo

Clinic, usually in a condition of crisis. Since Episcopalians are a group of Christians who view the sacraments as a means whereby we receive God's healing grace, they expect and deserve this ministry."

That same year, the chaplain's office was moved to Calvary Church. Rev. Crowle used a pager and a telephone answering service to keep in touch with patients at St. Marys. Support from Calvary was more than moral: the parish helped supplement the chaplaincy budget in the areas of continuing education, vacation replacement, and travel allowance.

Growing Interest in Spirituality and Healing

By the mid-1980s, the ecumenical scene had brightened considerably. An expansion at St. Marys provided for a new chaplains' facility near the west entrance. Protestants had formerly worshiped in the small chapel. But in 1984, Rev. Crowle reported, "we worship in the large and beautiful St. Marys Chapel sharing service times with our Roman Catholic friends and telecasting the service around the hospital in black and white, but soon they say, in color." That same year, St. Marys employed a new chaplain as Protestant Coordinator; never before had any but a Roman Catholic been on the staff. Meanwhile, the full-time denominational chaplains, funded by their faith communities, began to stay overnight when on 24-hour call three times a month.

Rev. Crowle retired as diocesan chaplain at the Mayo Medical Center in 1988. That same year, the Mayo Foundation bought St. Marys and Methodist hospitals, and merged their separate chaplaincy departments. The religious traditions of both St. Marys and Methodist hospitals required Mayo to come to grips in an officially supportive way with the pastoral dimensions of patient care. Rev. Crowle's expressed hopes began to bear fruit. His wish for a serious re-engagement of medicine and religion also came to pass in the Mayo Foundation's increased interest in the interface between spirituality and healing.

Rev. Crowle's successor, the Rev. Martin W. Pfab, served as Episcopal chaplain in 1988 and 1989, when he became part of the new Mayo Chaplaincy Department. Rev. Pfab had served as a Roman Catholic priest before coming to the Episcopal Church. Upon his appointment as a staff chaplain in Mayo's newly established department, the Diocese of Minnesota eliminated the position of denominational chaplain. Rev. Pfab had a particular gift for ministry with the dying and by preference took charge of the night chaplain's work. Although he was a Mayo chaplain for most of his tenure, with primary duties to the patient population at large, he continued to minister to Episcopalians out of his own commitment to them. His devotion was much appreciated. "To be able to provide a consistent high quality reliable patient pastoral care program that is uniquely Episcopalian is indeed a great honor," he wrote in his 1989 report. "The ecumenical responsibilities of working together are daily more interesting."

With the presence of Rev. Pfab as a Mayo chaplain, Episcopalians at Mayo continued to receive pastoral care. Rev. Pfab's efforts were supplemented by pastoral care from the rectors of Calvary and St. Luke's and from Calvary's deacons, dedicated lay volunteers and other area clergy. The need for specialized training for clergy and lay volunteers in confidentiality and patients' rights, and increasing requests from patients for pastoral care, became issues at the medical center.

Episcopal Pastoral Services

In the spring of 1998, the Rev. Nick Mezacapa, rector of Calvary Church, and the Rev. Steve Mues, rector of St. Luke's, established an advisory board consisting of members from both parishes. The mission was to establish a more organized way of providing an Episcopal connection to patients at the two hospitals. With cooperation from the Department of Chaplain Services at Mayo Medical Center and funding through a grant from the Diocese of Minnesota, the mission was accomplished through what became the Episcopal Pastoral Services.

Episcopal Pastoral Services is designed to provide visits by Episcopalian lay persons and clergy to patients and their families at the two Mayo hospitals. Alternating every two weeks, volunteers from the churches visit patients daily, Monday through Friday. The primary source of patient names is hospital admittance forms, supplemented by referrals from parishes and families. While most patients are from Minnesota and surrounding states, others come from around the U.S. and the world, encompassing the entire Anglican Communion.

Currently, volunteers are trained as Lay Eucharistic Visitors and are able to take the sacrament to those who request it. In addition, Rev. Mezacapa of Calvary and the Rev. Doug Sparks, the current rector of St. Luke's, can be relied on when a clergy visit is requested. The goal is to accommodate the needs of fellow Episcopalians hospitalized in Rochester and to be friends in Christ to those who come for healing. The ministry that began eighty years ago with the beloved Father Brown remains vital as Calvary continues into the 21st century.

Jan Larson

Chapter 12

Fruitcake

By Jan Larson

Once upon a time, in 1939, a Calvary parishioner named Mabel Henderson gathered several of her church friends (Anna Pemberton, Ethel New, Nell Crenshaw and Frances Berkman) in her kitchen to make fruitcake. The ladies made the fruitcakes with Mrs. Henderson's recipe and sold them at Calvary. These humble beginnings launched the great Calvary Church fruitcake tradition.

The 1939 project was a big hit and moved from Mrs. Henderson's kitchen to her basement the following year where some 200 cakes were made. The basement wasn't really big enough to handle all of this, so the decision was made to move the operation to the church itself. Calvary's kitchen was very old at the time, and someone said they didn't know how anything could be done in "this unbelievable place," with the old black, gas stove. But, they persevered. The money from the sales of the cakes was put into a savings account for Calvary. Before Mrs. Henderson died in 1959, she gave the entire account, $20,000, to be used for the remodeling of a new kitchen.

In 1959, Peg Hargesheimer, who was president of Calvary Episcopal Churchwomen (CEC), then called Ladies' Parish Aid, had a conversation with Eleanor Kirklin saying they would probably have to drop the fruitcake project because Mrs. Henderson had died. Eleanor said they couldn't do that because the women had worked too hard all those twenty years making $1,000 a year. Although she had never been involved with fruitcake, having lived away from Rochester, Eleanor said she was back now and would help keep it going. Eleanor pooled other parishioners: Rae Doty, Betsy Hilker, Anna Pemberton and Grace Markham to help her get organized. And so they did.

"Where's the Butter?"

However, on the first day of baking, someone asked, "Where's the butter?" It hadn't been creamed or anything. Eleanor said she didn't know about creaming butter and sugar. They did bake 75 pounds that first day, and she said it was the greatest struggle of anything she'd ever done. Today we make at least 425 pounds the first day. Eleanor said that back then, they always made a special five-pound cake because Mrs. Kruse, of Kruse Lumber, always sent one as a gift to Bernard Baruch, the Wall Street financier who advised President Franklin Roosevelt and was a friend of Mrs. Kruse's.

Eventually, the women made seven different sized cakes. Today, we make nine sizes. The project seemed to grow each year. One year, we made 86 batches, but those were the days when more than half the churchwomen showed up to volunteer. As women entered the workforce, our number of volunteers declined. We finally had to put a limit on how many batches we made, and today, we limit it to sixty to sixty-three batches.

Fruitcake preparation, 1964. Clockwise from left: Peg Ackerman, Vera Engle, Virginia Vaughn, Ginny Shick, Nell Crenshaw, Frances Berkman, Gertrude Christenson.

Back in the early 1970s, Eleanor asked me to assist her, so this began my "on the job" training, and we two worked side by side for many years. We had an address book or "order book," as we called it. It was this book that we used to send letters to people who had bought cakes the year before. As the price of postage rose, we resorted to postcards, and today we send out 300 to 400 cards with all the information for ordering by phone, letter, or e-mail. Today, we list the cakes on the church website. The notices include the price of cakes, the information for special orders, how to have cakes mailed, and when the cakes will be available for pick-up.

Before Eleanor gave up the helm, we started duplicating the book orders on the computer because some of the orders were getting confusing for her. I remember that when the Rev. Larry Bussey, assistant to the Rev. Sam Cook, suggested that we start putting the orders on a computer, Eleanor's blood pressure rose a couple of digits. She did *not* like computers. So, she stuck with her order book, and the office used the computer. I guess it's a generational thing.

Another thing we had to get used to, and this was because of engineering innovations, was the convection oven. Earlier, I mentioned the old black gas stove. It had one small and one big oven. There were days when, having started at 6:00 a.m., we wouldn't leave church until 6 p.m. because of a backlog of cakes that needed to be baked. The committee organized to purchase a new stove had some conflicting ideas. Some wanted to continue with gas; others wanted to go electric. However, the argument that electricity was safer won because with gas, a child might go through the kitchen and accidentally turn on a knob which of course would turn on the gas. Our committee settled on the present stove in the kitchen. None of us had been exposed to convection ovens, but we decided, as we did with other things, that we would take our chances, roll with the punches, and make the best of it because we hoped that the convection ovens would speed up the process. And they did! By the way, Michael's Restaurant in Rochester bought the old black gas stove.

Another adjustment we have had to make is to the steamers, or "roasters," as some refer to them. When the project first began, there were two steamers; now, we have fifteen or sixteen of them, each donated to the church. We used to have a repair person who could take the old roasters and fix them when they wore out, but eventually parts were unable to be purchased, and they were unable to be repaired. We were in need of more of them and glad when they were finally being produced again. We miss the old ones because cakes were easier to place in them for the steaming process. The new ones aren't as roomy, so again we roll with the punches and adjust, but sometimes with little burns on our forearms.

A Place for Everything

It is often said that you can't teach an old dog new tricks, and sometimes that is true. We have gone with the flow when it's the best way to go, but there are certain things that have never changed. For instance, if you come into the kitchen during the baking process, you'll notice all the roasters on the counters have names on them. You might recognize these names by past and present parishioners. They are referred to by: "Buie," "Carpenter," or "Randall," etc. They have had the same place on the counter for as long as I can remember. When the roasters die, they are replaced by a newer model but keep the name.

When the Oasis Building project started in the early 2000s, I asked the building committee to include storage space for the roasters. We had cubbyholes built in the basement near the undercroft. Each cubby holds one roaster, and you can see the roaster's name. Some people think it looks kind of like a crypt for roasters.

I would like to comment about the wax-paper liners that fit in the tins. When I first became involved, we had women sitting in Brackenridge Hall all day long doing nothing more than cutting and folding paper. Each tin has a specific length of wax paper for its size. There is only one size pan that has ever given us production problems — the 1 ½ lb. tins. We have only twenty 1 ½ lb. tins. Eleanor said we had to do three batches of the 1 ½ lb. tins a day. That means sixty 1 ½ lb. cakes. We used to be here forever because, after they were steamed and baked, we had to cool the tin, send the tins to Brackenridge to have more liners made, send back to the kitchen, fill, steam, and bake and repeat again. The 1 ½ lb. cakes are the first to begin our day. Fifteen to twenty years ago, I started having people come in ahead of the baking to cut and fold the wax paper. We put them in boxes until they were ready to use. This really sped up the process. We no longer had to wait for certain sizes to be made. Now, some people start cutting wax paper during the winter months to have something to do on snowbound days. But still today we begin the 6:00 a.m. shift with twenty 1 ½ lb. cakes. Our goal is to have them in the steamers by 6:30 a.m. We are finished now by 3 p.m.

Recently, a number of men and youth have joined the ranks of the women workers and have earned the gratitude and appreciation of all, which makes a truism of the old adage "many hands make light work." We now are referred to as the Fruitcake Committee.

From Mailing Lists to the Chicken Dance:
A Year-Round Process

In the order of things, there seems to be no real beginning or end. After the cakes are sold out and everything is organized and put away, we begin updating our mailing list for the following year. In May or June the fruit is ordered for later delivery. The dates arrive in July, and we begin cutting, weighing and bagging them. In September the dried fruit (raisins, currants, etc.) are weighed and bagged. In the time of Mrs. Henderson, the raisins used to have to be washed and dried on cheesecloth before being used. Measuring the flour and spices is done a couple of weeks before baking. Mixing all the weighed fruit with the "fruit supreme" is done the week before. This is probably the messiest part of the fruitcake process. During the mixing, raisins fall on the floor, syrup and other stuff spills, people walk through it, and shoes stick and make noise with every step we take. Now, we bring a rag mop into the kitchen. We are kind of like dogs scratching backwards to wipe our sticky shoes off. After all the fruit ingredients are mixed together, they are stored in five-gallon buckets to "cure," awaiting the next order of business which is the actual batter process.

Photo by Julie Roenigk

Fruitcake decorating, 2006. From left: Barbara Senjem, Claire Heins, Cindy Heins, Nancy Dingel, Kay Karsell, Ines Mathieson.

Around this time, the steamers are brought upstairs and set on the kitchen counters and on tables that line the hallway outside the kitchen. That is the sign to the parish that fruitcake preparation is moving into high gear.

The day before baking, someone creams enough butter and sugar for the batches to be baked that day. Being at room temperature makes it easy to blend into the fruit mixture. After eggs, flour and spices are added, the batter is ready to be put in tins and await the steaming process. Charts are put over each roaster with "time in" and "time out" because the steaming time depends on the size of the cake. The same goes for the baking of the cakes. The steamer position is very important. Soon, the beautiful aroma of fruitcake fills the church.

There are many teams at work, some in the kitchen, the center of operations where mixing and measuring occurs. About fifteen to twenty years ago, we started wearing blue surgical hats to prevent hair from getting into mixtures. Indispensable to this process are those who cut and fold the wax paper that lines the baking tins in all their various sizes. After the cakes are steamed and baked to perfection, they are placed on trays, taken to another area to be trimmed and glazed by yet another team. The decorators then swing into action with all the creativity they can muster to give each cake its crowning glory and festive design. Cindy Heins makes all the calls to set up the decorator schedule.

Virginia Vaughn and Jerry Korstad

Photo by Julie Roenigk

The next process is undertaken by the wrapping team. After the cakes have cooled overnight, they are neatly wrapped in Saran wrap and placed in the storage cupboards by size, waiting to be sold. The final day of wrapping the cold cakes calls for a celebration. The paper is ripped from the tables and a version of the chicken dance is done by Carol Lamberg, retired office manager, and anyone who wishes to join her.

The last team, marketing, gets the orders ready locally and for mailing. I mentioned postcards were mailed out to former buyers; two big signs are also placed on strategic corners of the church indicating "famous fruitcake" for sale. Many Mayo Clinic patients stop and make purchases. Occasionally, a newspaper article helps to push sales. In the times when CEC had their bazaar, people lined up on the street waiting to get in to buy fruitcake. It was not unusual for the line to be a block long. One year, the *Post-Bulletin* wrote an article, and the cakes sold like hotcakes. I told Eleanor that we better not sell any more before the bazaar because we had advertised to sell cakes. We had about only about fifteen to twenty cakes to sell, and believe me, the public was very unhappy.

We have found it advantageous to be open for business on the last Saturdays in November and the first ones in December. The last couple of years we have taken part in the Shorewood Senior Complex Boutique in November. This has become a very profitable endeavor.

Several years ago, I decided to experiment — I had heard some people say they loved fruitcake but couldn't eat it because they were celiac. I got a couple of people to help me make a half batch of gluten-free cakes. I called the people, sold them two for one, and wanted an evaluation. We now get enough special orders to bake at least one batch. This is the last batch on the last day of baking. The cakes are identified because we insert a toothpick in each cake. That toothpick gets steamed, baked, glazed and decorated. It is removed in the wrapping process and a special ribbon is attached to the cake.

A Ton of Fruitcake, Now Digitally Weighed

You might be interested in the inventory chart which I included for the past five years. We make over a ton of fruitcake each year, 2,000 pounds, which becomes 1,500 to 1,900 cakes depending on the sizes we make. About ten years ago we started using a digital scale. We used to eyeball the old scales, and everyone read them differently. We always put an extra dab on to make sure we weren't shorting the weight. The first year of the new scale we made over 100 extra cakes because of the precision weighing, using the same amount of batter.

Cake Count

Size	2003	2004	2005	2006	2007	2008
1/2 lb. loaf	504	577	596	584	607	680
1 lb. loaf	686	674	660	656	643	712
1 1/2 lb. loaf	280	251	249	258	285	319
2 lb. loaf	199	151	157	160	190	213
2 lb. round	47	36	42	48	47	53
3 lb. loaf	27	19	21	31	39	44
3 lb. round	6	4	3	4	6	7
5 lb. loaf	0	1	1	4	1	3
5 lb. round	1	0		1	2	1
TOTAL	1750	1711	1729	1747	1820	2032

Fruitcake Fit for a Queen – and a First Lady

Our fruitcakes have gone far and wide. Once, former First Lady Barbara Bush was in town. She is an Episcopalian. We had a friend set up a meeting so I could give her a fruitcake. I was a little nervous when the Secret Service agents stared at me over their newspapers as I arrived. But Mrs. Bush and I had a nice visit, and I received a lovely note. We have even given a fruitcake to Queen Noor of Jordan.

Fruits of Our Labors

Fruitcake profits have contributed to a variety of causes. I'll just mention the major ones. In 1961, $500 was pledged to the church's operating fund. These contributions have continued to increase over the years. Since 1961, a total of $145,000 has been given to the operating budget.

Other Projects Funded by Fruitcake Sales:

1981	$5,000 copy machine for office; $2,000 interior church painting
1990	$3,700 restore and install Gothic stained glass window in ambulatory
1994	$5,900 re-facing the kitchen cupboards and new linoleum
1995	$6,600 copy machine for office; $1,700 booster heater for dishwasher; $3,000 ceiling lights for Brackenridge Hall
1998	$6,500 new dishwasher
2000	$2,000 initiated a fund for the elevator

2002 $3,000 new fridge for kitchen

2004 $5,250 stained glass window in west entry

2005 $5,000 Certificate of Deposit to maintain Oasis Garden

2007 $3,200 28 chairs for Crawford Hall;
        $1,900 for the Episcopal cross on the west side of the building

Until 2006 at least $1,000 yearly was donated for outreach to local non-profit organizations.

From Age to Age

There is a small fruitcake buried in the cornerstone of the new addition to Calvary. The original recipe, on a grease-stained card, remains in the Calvary safe. The tradition of fruitcake baking for sales prior to Christmas has carried on from the early 20th century and now into the 21st century — one generation of "hands" having passed expertise to another generation. It inspires a spirit of devotion, enthusiasm, pride and fellowship for the women, men and youth involved. So, "it takes many hands do make light work," and hopefully this project will carry on happily ever after.

> *"They do not die who leave their thoughts imprinted on*
> *some deathless page; they pass, but the work they wrought*
> *lives from age to age."*

Laying the cornerstone at the Calvary Mission Church, Oct. 30, 1960. From left: Samuel Allen, Calvary parishioner; the Rt. Rev. Hamilton Kellogg, bishop of Minnesota; the Rev. O. Wendell McGinnis, rector of Calvary; and the Rev. Peter Paulson, curate at Calvary.

164

Chapter 13

Calvary and St. Luke's

By Joseph A. Gibilisco and Marvin W. Heins *

"Calvary will not move, Calvary will not sell. Calvary stays right where it is."

-- The Rt. Rev. Hamilton Kellogg,
Bishop of Minnesota
August 1958

The Bishop's decision brought a guarded smile and big sigh of relief to about half of us, and took the wind right out of the sails of the other half. In the next few years, nine other churches would move out of downtown — Calvary was one of only a handful that stayed. But as his statement shut one door, it also opened a small window, a window of opportunity — may we say, "God's window?"

Rochester would someday have a second Episcopal Church, and Calvary would be its mother. It all makes good sense, now; but back then? It wasn't all that easy.

The authors are former members of Calvary and founding members of St. Luke's Episcopal Church.

Back in the 1950s

May we back up a few years to the mid-1950s? Calvary Church was becoming old and jammed to the rafters with newer, younger members who had kids — lots and lots of kids. Every inch of space in the church, in Brackenridge Hall, the former sexton's house, and the old rectory was put to use—even the kitchen, boiler room, and rector's office held Sunday School classes. We briefly considered renting Sunday School space from nearby St. John's School. As early as 1952, the demands of growth were mentioned at the annual meeting and the vestry was instructed to begin planning for a time when the crowded conditions would warrant expanding Calvary or finding a new location.

The following year, Mayo Clinic completed construction and occupancy of the Mayo Building with considerable additions to the staff of physicians, scientists, nurses, and allied health and administrative personnel. Shortly thereafter, in 1956, IBM announced that it would establish a Rochester facility with an addition of approximately 7,000 to 8,000 employees, including engineers and support staff. Hence, not only was Calvary's membership growing, but the community itself was experiencing an expansion that continues to this day.

It was on May 2, 1957, that Mayo Clinic made its fateful proposal. It offered to buy Calvary's downtown location for $261,500 outright or to pay $187,000 plus a piece of land between Third and Fourth Streets SW, facing Eighth Avenue across from the Foundation House. Note that the proposed purchase amount of $261,500 was, at that time, considered most generous.

At a specially called parish meeting held in the church, on May 14, 1957, the second offer was approved. It needed two-thirds of the votes, and received that, but just barely. The vestry now had permission from the congregation to accept Mayo's second offer.

Then the Fun Began ...

A vocal and zealous "Committee for the Preservation of the Downtown Church" quickly formed. Litigation became a possibility because of a lack of clarity in the existing state law pertaining to the sale of church property. The vestry wisely backed away from the plan to sell the property to give it further consideration.

A new possible location, "The Baihly Farm," was then studied. The farm was farther out southwest, along the old beltline, on what was then the edge of town. It was in the area of the present Congregational United Church of Christ near Highway 52. We could have three times the building space, ten times the parking, and $261,500 to help get started. That plan was rejected at another specially called parish meeting on June 17, 1958.

Frustration was rampant. Members who loved and were devoted to Calvary felt threatened. Younger, more recent members, generally loyal, worried over the inadequate facilities necessary to accommodate the growing number of parishioners with school-age youngsters. The fear of losing an historic and well-loved building had to be balanced against fear of losing young families if the crowding issue was not resolved.

The Rev. O. Wendell McGinnis

Now, a few, but most necessary words about our rector, the Rev. O. Wendell McGinnis. He came from St. Paul's Episcopal Church in Duluth where he had been rector for the previous eleven years. He arrived in Rochester on October 1, 1954 — the hand-picked candidate of Bishop Keeler to lead Calvary through its growing pains. It was a good pick. However, we made his life difficult -- all of us. He was beset on all sides by excited partisans. Intentionally and firmly neutral, his door was open to one and all. He was a good listener, friendly and calm. He led us even when we didn't want to be led. No list of saints contains the name Wendell, but there ought to be one! His only voiced opinion was that when the decision was finally made, we would all come together for the good of the Church. He died too soon, on August 7, 1965, of cancer, long before he could see the fruits of his leadership.

The Decision

The Bishop opposed the sale of Calvary, but agreed that expanded growth justified establishing a second church. An extensive parish survey and questionnaire was sent to 515 parishioners. It read:

> *Dear Members and Friends of Calvary Church:*
>
> *The rector, assistant rector, wardens, and vestrymen of Calvary Episcopal Church have as their basic interest the prosperity and progress of our church. We feel that this interest is shared by all parishioners. Because we share this desire for progress, it was felt proper and necessary to solicit your views on an important matter pertaining to our church. Since the information*

obtained by this means may well have a decided effect upon the future course of this church, it is essential that each member make a sincere effort to complete and return the questionnaire this week. We ask, also, that you sign this questionnaire secure in the realization that all replies are considered confidential. Your vestry appreciates your guidance and help. This is your church, and your participation will determine its future.

Wendell McGinnis	*Lee Hargesheimer*
Robert D. Fenwick	*Garland C. Younger*
Robert W. Cross	*J.A. Gibilisco*
G.G. Stilwell, M.D.	*E. W. Johnson*
Eleanor J. Kirklin	*John Voskuil*
R. E. Campbell	*George F. Waters*
Archie Ackerman	

The vestry received 239 completed questionnaires, a response rate of 46 percent. The following is a summary of the opinions expressed:

For expansion now:	40 percent.
Against expansion:	32 percent
No opinion:	18 percent
For expansion later:	10 percent

Further analysis of the answers revealed that the number of communicants who preferred to attend each location were:

Calvary:	232 (49.7%)
Mission Church:	235 (50.3%)

The vestry's interpretation was that there should be two parishes so as to satisfy both groups. There was confidence that a mission could and should be established and that it would ultimately become a second parish. Although there was a great deal of controversy and some anger among the congregation's membership, the truth was that all sides did agree — the Calvary Church facility was inadequate to fill the needs of a vital growing parish.

It became clear that Calvary would not accept either of Mayo's offers, so the vestry sent a letter to Mr. Blackmun at Mayo Clinic — the same Mr. Blackmun who later in life would be known as Mr. Justice (Harry) Blackmun, serving on the United States Supreme Court for 24 years and best known for his lead opinion in *Roe v. Wade*. The letter to The Mayo Foundation on July 20, 1958 read:

> *Dear Mr. Blackmun:*
>
> *At a general meeting of the parish of Calvary Episcopal Church, Rochester, on June 17, 1958, a proposed resolution to sell the present church property was defeated. At a subsequent meeting of the vestry of the church, the vestrymen affirmed this action and asked me, as clerk, to inform the Mayo Association that the parish does not wish at this time to take advantage of the offer of the Mayo Association to purchase the church property. Your letter of May 21, 1958, to Dr. Philip Brown, Senior Warden of the church, noted the price of $261,500 and outlined the conditions upon which the sale was contingent. The vestry of Calvary Church deeply appreciates the courtesy, thoughtfulness and cooperation extended by the members of the Mayo Association in the negotiations for the proposed sale.*
>
> *Very truly yours,*
> *George G. Stilwell*
> *Clerk of the Vestry*
> *Calvary Episcopal Church*

The larger community was made aware that Calvary Episcopal Church was going to establish a second Episcopal location in Rochester. *The Rochester Post-Bulletin* informed the community by publishing the following on June 18, 1958:

> *Members of the Calvary Episcopal Church of Rochester have voted*
> *to retain the present church site and building but also decided to establish*
> *a parochial mission, the Rev. O. Wendell McGinnis, rector, announced.*
> *The votes were taken at a special parish meeting Tuesday night in*
> *North Hall of Mayo Civic Auditorium.*
>
> *The vestry will now proceed to look at possible sites and to make plans*
> *for a parochial mission building, which will be used for regular services*
> *for part of the congregation because of the overcrowded*
> *conditions at the present church. The mission will be under the direction*
> *of the Calvary Episcopal Church but could develop into a parish of*
> *its own in the future, Rev. McGinnis explained.*

In the resolution whether to sell the present church and property was the consideration of a new church site on the Baihly farm just southwest of Rochester across the beltline highway on the Salem or Mayowood Road. That site was turned down in the voting.

Bishop Kellogg was called to meet with the Calvary vestry. In August 1958 he advised us that he had followed closely and had carefully considered the many deliberations and controversial issues that were being discussed by the congregation. He was equally forceful in advising the vestry that the rector, assistant rector, and staff would remain intact. Further, the clergy would be supported throughout construction of the second facility as well as the renovation of Calvary Church. Having made those points clear, Bishop Kellogg then insisted that there be one budget for both Calvary and the Mission which would provide funds for future planning and maintenance.

A fundraising committee was formed. A professional consultant, The Wells Company of Minneapolis, was hired to manage the effort. Some $285,000 was pledged. Dr. Edward Henderson and Mr. Robert Roesler were assigned the task of locating a site for the mission. They found 4 ½ acres, a cornfield at the time, on the then-northwest edge of town and bought it.

Once again, the *Post-Bulletin* published its interpretation of the local Episcopal church deliberations.

> *The Vestry of the Calvary Episcopal Church announced today that work on remodeling of the downtown church and on construction of a new mission church building in northwest Rochester will begin next week.*
>
> *Contracts have been signed with Weis Builders Inc., for the downtown work, and with O. A. Stocke & Co. for the mission church building. Architect for both projects is the firm of McEnary & Kraff, Minneapolis, in association with Ellerbe & Co.*
>
> *The site of the new mission church is in the Hutchinson-Sauer addition in northwest Rochester, west of the International Motel. Work on the downtown church will be completed in about four months and the new mission church will be completed in about eight months.*

The downtown project includes a new sacristy, a new kitchen and new church school rooms in Brackenridge Hall, enclosing of the east porch, new toilets and lounge, new west entrance, structural strengthening, new electrical service and new furnace and heating system for the nave.

The mission building will have gothic Indiana and rubble stone on the exterior, with rubble stone and white oak paneling for the nave. The narthex will have quarry tile floor while the altar will be marble and the sanctuary floor will be stone.

Church school rooms below the nave will have vinyl-asbestos tile floors, block walls and red oak trim. Pews, organ, church school furniture, parking lot and landscaping are not included in the contract.

Planning guidelines for the future growth were identified, which would ultimately result in the establishment of a strong second Episcopal Church in Rochester. The subcommittee of the Calvary vestry, chaired by Wes Johnson, with guidance from clergy, identified the steps necessary for establishing a parochial mission. The steps are identified in Canon Law for the Diocese of Minnesota: A parish plants a mission in a new location; the parish's wardens and vestry hold the title to all real estate and funds until the mission is sufficiently large and financially stable to function independently. The mission congregation transforms into a parish congregation by becoming a religious corporation in the state of Minnesota and seeking union with the Episcopal Convention of the Diocese of Minnesota. The new parish can then elect its own wardens and vestry at its first annual meeting, hold title to its real estate and funds, choose a name, and call its own rector. Rev. McGinnis, the wardens, and vestry carefully followed all of these canonical and legal procedures. The creation of two independent parishes in Rochester, however, split the membership of Calvary with the disunion felt in both congregations.

We recall with considerable gratitude the effort that Rev. McGinnis and the Rev. Robert Fenwick, assistant rector, made to conduct services at both facilities. The Reverends McGinnis and Fenwick would both celebrate the 8:00 a.m. service downtown, then rush to the Mission for the 9:00 a.m. service. If one would stand in the parking lot following the 9:00 a.m. Mission Church service, both priests and the choir could be seen with their clerical garments intact racing across the parking lot and getting in cars to rush downtown for the 10:15 service at Calvary. (9:00 and 10:15 a.m. were identical). Calvary continued to sustain the young evolving mission as well as advancing its own growth.

From Parochial Mission to Parish: St. Luke's Episcopal Church

The Parochial Mission parish membership completed the necessary steps for establishing a diocesan church. The steps included having at least ninety members and a budget adequate for all obligations, selecting a church name, and completing the Articles of Incorporation and another document referred to as a General Agreement. Many people worked long and hard beginning in October 1963, and everything was ready on time. Title passed from the "Rector, Wardens, and Vestrymen of Calvary Episcopal Church, Rochester" to "St. Luke's Episcopal Church, Rochester, Minnesota" on January 2, 1964. The combined total indebtedness of both properties was calculated, and St. Luke's assumed 80 percent, and in turn gave a 20-year mortgage to the Rochester Building and Loan Association,

Mr. William Shedd, President. (Bill was a member of the new St. Luke's.)
St. Luke's called the assistant rector, Rev. Fenwick, a Lake City native
whose father had once been Calvary's choirmaster, as its first rector.

The St. Luke's parish petition for Union with the Diocese of
Minnesota was approved by Bishop Kellogg and the diocesan convention
on January 27, 1964. The petition was presented by Rev. Fenwick, Marvin
Heins, John Voskuil, and Joseph Gibilisco.

The "Naming Committee" had placed three names in nomination:
St. Luke's, St. Matthew's, and St. Thomas. St. Luke's was chosen.

> October has important significance to St. Luke's:
>
> 1. Mission cornerstone was laid on October 30, 1960.
> 2. The first service was held on October 6, 1961.
> 3. The service of dedication was held on October 30, 1961.
> 4. St. Luke's Day (Patronal Feast Day) is celebrated on October 18.

The first St. Luke's vestry consisted of: The Rev. Robert D. Fenwick,
rector; E.W. Johnson, Jr., senior warden; J.A. Claydon, junior warden;
Mrs. H.J. (Alice) Tashjian, E.J. Klampe, G.M. Laedtke, T.G. Martens, J.A.
Gibilisco, J.F. Voskuil, M.G. Brataas, Jr., D.A. Leonard, R.E. Campbell,
vestry members.

It was time to mend whatever injury had resulted following this
fourteen-year struggle and get on with the work that God sent us to do.
We did and we have. Joint ventures between St. Luke's and Calvary
continue to strengthen our mutual goals and the presence of the Episcopal
Church in Rochester. They include joint services on Ash Wednesday and
Thanksgiving Eve (with the location alternating between the parishes), a
combined Vacation Bible School, a weekly Education for Ministry seminar

which includes members of both parishes, and coordinated efforts for the Episcopal hospital chaplaincy in which members of both Calvary and St. Luke's serve Episcopalians at Mayo's hospitals. Finally, both rectors share in serving at the Thursday morning worship service with Eucharist at Charter House, a retirement home in Rochester.

Both Calvary and St. Luke's rejoice that two vibrant established Episcopal churches provide a spiritual home to so many. And may we add that Rochester and the Episcopal Church are much the better for it.

ADDENDUM

Just as Calvary extended the mission of the Episcopal Church into suburban Rochester in the 20th century, St. Luke's in the 21st century has extended the mission into the once rural Kasson. In 2008, St. Luke's and St. Peter's, Kasson, shared the stipend of the Rev. Justin Chapman, who is providing ministry services to both congregations with the rector of St. Luke's, the Rev. Douglas Sparks. The spirit of community that inspired Calvary's early clergy to provide services and pastoral care to small towns around Rochester continues to guide the work of the Episcopal Church in southeastern Minnesota.

178

Chapter 14

Slices of Calvary Life

A Calvary Childhood: Open-faced Sandwiches and Forts on the Lawn

By Timothy Hallett

Tim Hallett is the youngest son of the Rev. Leslie William Hallett, who served as Episcopal chaplain to the Mayo Clinic hospitals from 1946 to 1965. The large Hallett family (five of seven children still living at home) resided in the half-timbered "Old Rectory" at 311 Third Ave. SW, adjacent to Calvary Church, from 1946 to 1952.

I was five years old when the family moved to Rochester in 1946. Although Rochester was still a small city at the time, my existence, given the location of the house we lived in, was remarkably urban. Across the street was a lovely park surrounding the old Central School, then owned by the Clinic and used for the Medical Museum. I was fascinated by the wax models of various operations and the displays of medical instruments and items retrieved from children's windpipes. On one side of the house was Calvary's spacious lawn, with lots of bushes and trees to serve as forts and castles and hiding places. On the other side was the old Virginia Hotel, much smaller and more modest than the Kahler, but like the Kahler, sporting a large red neon sign on the roof. On summer evenings, guests at the Virginia would sit in lawn chairs on the sidewalk in front of the hotel. I enjoyed racing my tricycle around the block and having them time my circuits.

Tim Hallett

The high school and junior college (where my older sisters enrolled) was just across Fourth Avenue; Central Junior High School where my sister Patricia enrolled was just another block distant. The post office was across First Street, the public library across busy Second Street, the Plummer Building and the Kahler just a block away. All around were many rooming houses and hotels, with downtown just steps away. I soon learned to navigate the downtown honeycomb of tunnels. At nine o'clock every evening, just at dusk in the summertime, there was a fifteen-minute carillon concert, always ending with a hymn from our very own hymnal, "The day thou gavest, Lord, has ended." There was no staying out to play after that.

Our family was warmly embraced by the people of Calvary. In April 1947 the women of the parish sponsored an open house with the Halletts as guests of honor. Frances Berkman and Daisy Plummer were co-chairmen in charge of arrangements. The Calvary Parish *Visitor* has a full account of churchwomen responsible for the event, including, as was customary in those days, notice of who poured. I always looked forward to parish receptions because of the delicious open-faced sandwiches the ladies made for them. On this occasion I ate too many of them. Some 300 guests attended, including Bishop Kemerer.

Our family entered into the life and worship of the parish, though my father often took Sunday services in the surrounding towns. I attended the Children's Service, conducted by Anna Pemberton in Brackenridge Hall. At some point in the proceedings we all paraded into "Big Church" behind a small processional cross.

At Christmas and Easter there were special children's services, with Mrs. Pemberton telling the story of the season on a large flannelboard. As I grew older, I joined Hazel B. Martin's Junior Choir and in time served as an acolyte. Like many a young person in Rochester, I also took piano lessons from the sometimes formidable but nonetheless endearing Miss Martin. I was able to keep tabs on all the activities around Calvary, checking in on the fruitcake making and preparations for the bazaar, visiting with the sexton, Mr. Seaman, and supervising the construction of the lych-gate.

The house had a large, book-lined study (there was a secret compartment in the bookshelf!), with its own entrance off the vestibule so that people could visit the chaplain without intruding on his family. People often came by for comfort or counsel. Sometimes they would visit with my parents in the living room. A back stairway made it possible for the family to come and go to their rooms without disturbing the visitors. My father had the natural pastor's gift of putting people at their ease. He could walk into a room, and its occupant would suddenly recognize the person he had been wanting to hear his confession.

From the attic window of the house on Third Avenue, I had a bird's-eye view of the construction of the Mayo Building (which we always called the "New Clinic"). In 1952, parish growth made it necessary to appropriate the Old Rectory for office and church school space. The diocese purchased a house on Eleventh Avenue SE as chaplain's residence, and my family moved into it, taking with us the happy memories of our life on Calvary's campus.

Pie Patrol: A Warm Welcome to Newcomers

By Jim Carlson

The Calvary Episcopal Pie Patrol started in the early 1990s. Like most of my ideas, it is not original. I got the idea while reading a magazine article that described how a church in another part of the country welcomed visitors by giving each of them baked goods.

This sounded like a very good idea. It would thank people for visiting. It would show that the church was genuinely interested in new members. It would encourage visitors to come again.

I spoke to Father Nick, and he agreed the idea had promise. We decided that the delivery of the pie would not be a drawn-out visit with a long presentation about the church and an appeal to join. The pie would be delivered simply with a short note thanking the person for visiting.

The Pie Patrol then began. I would get the list of visitors from Carol Lamberg (Calvary's office manager at the time) on Tuesday or Wednesday. I would then go through the drive-thru window at Baker's Square to pick up an assortment of apple pies. The thought was that apple is the most popular pie, so we could not go wrong with apple. I then dropped off the pies and a short note to the visitors from the previous Sunday. This was before the days of MapQuest and the GPS units. I had to study the Rochester street map before each trip.

After a while the Pie Patrol Committee was formed so that each visitor got a homemade pie instead of a Baker's Square pie. The baking of the pies is spread out among the many volunteers, who choose what kind of pie they want to bake. In addition to a homemade pie, visitors now get a folder with information about the church.

"Promoting Sociability":
Calvary's First Youth Group, circa 1912

By Barbara Toman

For anyone who has organized a youth group, the surviving records of the Young Peoples Guild make instructive reading. Written in elegant script by secretary Rodney Waldron, the group's notebook devotes nearly as many pages to the Constitution and By Laws as to actual business. The group's structure was complex. According to Constitution Article I (2), the guild was to consist of two "divisions": "the senior, to be known as Company A, and the Juniors, Company B or St. Margaret's Guild." Company A would consist of all members over the age of twenty; Company B, all members under twenty and "the members of Dr. and Mrs. Graham's classes." Each company would have its own "captain."

The "object of the Y.P.G." was to be "(1) The Advancement of the Interests of the Church" and "(2) The Promotion of sociability among the members." The guild would meet on the first Tuesday of each month, and the companies "fortnightly on alternate Tuesdays from September to June." According to By Laws Article I (2), the company meetings "will be informal and shall be devoted to sociability, under direction of Company Captains."

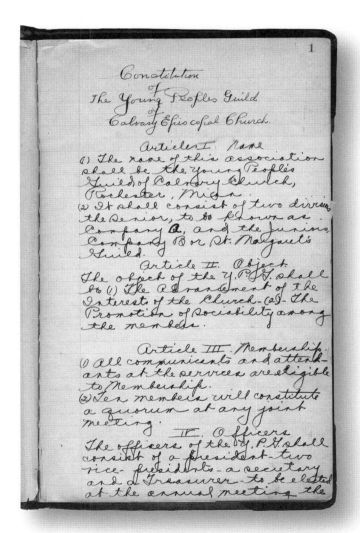

The Constitution and By-Laws of the Young People's Guild, as noted by Rodney Waldron.

Each member was expected to pledge "a voluntary offering of at least one dollar each semester." That must have been a substantial sum, for the "funds of the Guild" were to be devoted to "Mission work of the Church, Xmas decorations, Choir Master's salary, New Music, Flowers for Members, and such other objects as may be decided by Majority Vote."

At its first meeting, on September 17, 1912, in the Parish House (Brackenridge Hall's predecessor), the twelve members present discussed finances and decided to throw a party for the parish on Friday, October 5. The guild's treasurer, Walter Rowley, resigned (no reason is given), so "Mr. John Haines was elected to fill the office." At the second meeting, on October 1, the major item discussed was what to serve at the party: "A committee consisting of Miss McDermott and Miss Ungemach and Edith Graham was appointed to solicit cakes." Rodney Waldron kept minutes of these meetings, his handwriting deteriorating slightly but still elegant enough.

Minutes of the next gathering, on October 22, are scrawled in black crayon: "The third meeting of the Young Peoples Guild was called to order by Mr. Wurtele at 8 PM – and as a quorum was not present, was adjourned till Oct. 29th."

Perhaps they were still recovering from the parish party. It must have been a huge success; the names and addresses of 124 attendees are listed in the guild's notebook. At the top of the list is Margaret Brackenridge, who would have been 82 years old. Among the others listed are Mr. and Mrs. Robert Waldron (Rodney's parents, presumably); Minnie and Maude McDermott (one of them on the cake committee); Hazel Ungemach and Edith Graham (also on the cake committee); Dr. and Mrs. Christopher Graham; and other names prominent in the parish.

The guild was back on track for its meeting on October 29. Rodney used a pencil to keep the minutes, and the group voted to host another party on November 22, in Woodman Hall. This party was to have an admission charge of 25 cents as well as an auction, with proceeds going to charity. A few days before the party, at a meeting on November 19, "Girls were appointed to ask the different members for donations of candy to be sold at auction." All members bringing candy or cake to the auction were to be excused the payment of admission.

This party also must have been a success because afterward, at the November 26 meeting, "It was decided to spend $15 on 6 baskets for the poor for Thanksgiving and it was also voted to buy three pairs of glasses for poor boys." In addition, "Mr. Wurtele was asked to buy Christmas decorations."

The minutes end there.

Fruitcake Tidbits: Seventy Years of Laughter and Goo

By Jan Larson

I asked a number of people for "tidbits" about fruitcake. I put an article in the Sunday church bulletin, I visited with some elderly parishioners, and the answer I got from most was, "I can't remember." Several people did respond, so I will include their remarks.

Evie Devine said she always hoped someone would drop a cake. Then it couldn't be sold, but we could eat it. Virginia Vaughn told me she wanted to go see a Nat King Cole concert fifty years ago, the night before baking, but Louie wouldn't let her because she'd get home too late. She was disappointed because Mrs. Hilker, almost ninety at the time, did go.

I remember the time (before cell phones) when my alarm didn't go off, and I was thirty minutes late opening the doors to the church. Marrieta Giles was quite upset with me. She spent all day breaking eggs and felt she was behind on her end of the job because of my tardiness. Since that time I have always set two alarms.

Ginger Knutson said Mrs. Weber always commented on her daughter's red shoes during the fruitcake season. And who can forget the wonderful, guttural chuckle of Helen Duncanson? Claire VanZant, decorator, describes her day-long partnership with bowls of sticky adhesive, viscous cherries dripping in glutinous "goo," candied pineapple and hot sugar glaze making you stick to your seat.

The Wednesday morning small group's champion decorator was Dr. Mary Fidler, a pathologist at Mayo Clinic. She could slice glace cherries paper-thin, and her decorations were a sight to behold. The Wednesday morning group also helped on a baking day. Barbara Toman recalls being handed a tray of fruitcakes to take to the steamers. She wasn't prepared for such a heavy load, and her knees buckled. For a panicky moment she thought she might drop the tray. Barbara remembers my telling her that Betty Holtegaard and Irene Colvin, who were at least thirty years older than she was, did this all day long. That same day, she was asked to log the fruitcakes in and out of the steamers and ovens. She was amazed at the intricacy of the operation—it was like a well-choreographed ballet, or maybe the D-Day landings.

Eleanor Kirklin's granddaughter, who moved back to Rochester from Pensacola, Florida, remembers a time at the Borders Bookstore down there. She happened to mention that she was from Rochester, Minnesota. A customer overheard her and said, "I remember fruitcakes from the Episcopal church in Rochester!"

David Kemmer always bows and kisses my hand, calling me "the fruitcake queen." He has to eat the gluten-free and is delighted we are making it.

We have kept track of all the excuses from people who couldn't help with making fruitcake. I was going to publish some of them, but decided not to, except for this one: "Not this year, call me next year." Well, we did call again and got the same response!

"To Quicken Boys and Girls in Love for the Lord"

By Barbara Toman

One gem in Calvary's archives is a small notebook, undated but possibly from the early 20th century, titled "Christian Nurture Series of Lessons: Pupil's Note Book." As stated on the cover, the aim of the lessons series was "to quicken boys and girls in love for the Lord Jesus Christ …" Next to "Name of Teacher" is faintly penciled *Gertrude Boynton*. Next to "Name of Scholar," *Gladys* is just legible; her last name too faded to read.

Bound by metal brads, the notebook appears designed for lessons to be added as a student completes them, although this particular book has just two pages. One of those pages has a sepia photograph of a child

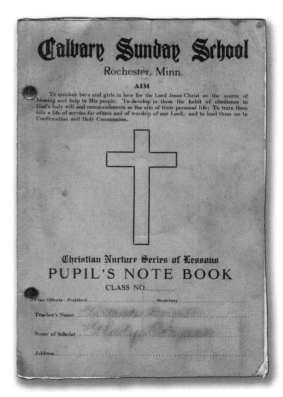

Gladys's notebook

kneeling with folded hands. Underneath, Gladys has carefully written: "This boy is praying. I think he is asking God to help him to be a good boy, and to do what is right."

Mrs. Boynton apparently liked Gladys's work. The notebook's back cover has a chart labeled "Calvary Sunday School Credits." Under "First Sunday," Gladys received twenty points in each of four categories: "Present"; "Punctual"; "Behavior"; and "Lesson Work." The rest of the Sundays on the chart are blank.

A Gift for the Mission: the Plummer Organ

By Joseph A. Gibilisco and Marvin W. Heins

The period when decisions were being made to set up the parochial mission that eventually became St. Luke's Episcopal Church in Rochester produced many small but interesting stories. One of them concerns Daisy Plummer, the widow of Dr. Henry Plummer. She had been a life-long parishioner at Calvary and had supported the parish's ministry as a member of the Berkman family. Indicating an interest in Calvary's parochial mission, she invited Drs. Ed Henderson and Herman Young to call upon her. After hearing their assurances that Calvary church would not be sold to Mayo, then, and only then, she offered her home pipe organ to the mission along with a generous stipend for moving, adaptation and installation. This was a most beautiful gift, of great value. The organ was made in 1913 for the Plummer House by the Aeolian Company. A gift to Dr. and Mrs. Plummer from Dr. Will Mayo, the organ had 35 stops and 21 ranks. It was dedicated at St. Luke's on March 31, 1963, by Bishop McNairy, and served St. Luke's for almost forty more years before needing replacement.

A Calvary Education: "Big Church" and "Little Church"

By Dulcie Berkman

I was baptized at Calvary Episcopal Church in March of 1946 after my father came home from World War II. I was fifteen months old. My earliest memory of Calvary is the day my mother enrolled my sister, Nancy, and me in Sunday School. We were warmly welcomed by Mrs. Martens, who was Nancy's teacher that year. I don't recall my teacher, but I do remember that we didn't go to church with the grownups before going to Sunday School. We had a separate service in what is now the choir room. It was set up with an altar, and I don't remember anything about the man who led the service except that he was robed as any minister would be.

This "Little Church," I soon learned, only went through third grade, and when I was in fourth grade I went into the "Big Church" with my mother. In those days, Morning Prayer and Holy Communion were held on alternating Sundays. On the days of Morning Prayer, we stayed for the entire service; on Holy Communion days, halfway into the service, all the Sunday School kids would leave to go to their respective classes. Some were held in the church building, others in the houses across the alley — the Seaman House on Fourth Avenue (which my sister and I called "the white house") and the Hallett House on Third Avenue across from what is now the Mayo Building. I have no recollection of what was on that block prior to 1955, the year the Mayo Building opened. Mrs. Peg Twentyman was my sixth grade teacher.

"Little Church," 1950s. Younger children had a separate worship service in Calvary's basement, in what is now the choir room.

The teen Sunday School class was taught by Mr. and Mrs. John Engelbert. This was an interesting class, for it was there that we learned about other faiths. As a group we went to services at other churches and would discuss the differences and similarities in our next Sunday School session. Our visit to the Greek Orthodox Church is the one I remember best. In one class we had an interesting discussion on how to handle the merging of several Protestant churches in the event that it ever happened.

From seventh grade to graduation, we had social events in a youth group called Young People's Fellowship, or as we called it, "YPF." We met on Sunday afternoons, and I especially remember the interdenominational events, one of which was a student-led church service. The other was attending an interdenominational convention of church youth groups in Minneapolis. The bus left from the Presbyterian Church in Rochester, and we stayed overnight in people's homes. I'd never been to a convention before. My mother even made a special dress for me to wear to the banquet! I remember the dress to this day. I feel fortunate to have experienced the many opportunities for spiritual growth, broadening experiences, and just plain fun that Calvary gave its young people.

Brian Williams seated at the Noehren-Harris organ, 2009.

Photo by Penny Duffy

"A French Organ with an English Soul"
By Brian A. Williams

Every pipe organ has a unique voice. Father Nick's description of our Noehren-Harris organ—"a French organ with an English soul"—is quite apt. The reed pipes, which sound like trumpets, are of a French Classic (or French

Baroque) design. Built in 1974, our organ is typical of others of that era in favoring "sparkle" more than heavy sounds. Tastes being what they are, a heavier sound is now preferred again! Because our room favors high pitches, one has to be very careful in registering the various sounds (i.e., which stops are drawn) so as not to be too bright for too long. The French Baroque reed pipes help punch out the lower pitches and also help keep the top notes from becoming too screechy, but are occasionally frustrating to use as solo sounds since they get softer as you go up the scale. That said, this organ is a very versatile instrument. You can make it sound English, if you try. The characteristics of an English organ are the really smooth sound and what's called the "large swell"—the part of the organ enclosed in a box with shutters. The organ's volume is controlled by gradually opening and closing the shutters. We have a fairly large swell division; our organ is in two chambers with full-length shutters that open and close. If all of a sudden you close the full swell with all the reeds blazing, it's like a muffled roar. But then you gradually open it up, and the roar starts again. It comes to life, with all its expression. That's the English style.

David Harris, who built our organ to Robert Noehren's specifications, is still building organ components that are considered some of the best in the industry. Amazingly, he built a lot of our organ's winding system from Air Force-surplus stainless steel. The stuff's indestructible, but was never meant to be used for a pipe organ. It's a very unique way of doing things, but it works.

Calvary's organ is a compromise in many ways. We have tried to stuff as many pipes as possible in one small area. There's a lot of room for small pipes but not for big ones, and the pipes are really close together. The organ's never going to be world-class, but, nonetheless, it always does what we want it to do.

There are some things I'd like to do someday, but they're expensive. It would be nice to have two sets of pipes in the back of the room: one set of "principals," that standard organ tone that would help bolster congregational singing in the back; and a big, solo, fanfare trumpet. That'd be really fun!

Fellowship Year-Round

By Frank Hawthorne

Over the century and a half of its existence, Calvary's parish life has revolved around the liturgical calendar followed by Christians everywhere since the first century. Without the discipline of worship and festival, and the fellowship they entail, we could not have survived, thrived, and remained relevant on this corner of the world. Many of our parish festivals are common among Anglicans: wreath-making on the first Sunday of Advent; tree-trimming and hanging greens in the church just before Christmas; the Shrove Tuesday pancake supper, prepared and served (under parental supervision) by Calvary youth to raise funds for their mission trips; and the post-Easter Vigil "Agape Meal." The latter was started in the 1980s by a group led by George Gorbatenko, an IBM employee who lent his Russian Orthodox heritage and superior cooking skills to the establishment of a great parish tradition (since then sustained by "Chef" Pat Moran and other stalwart volunteers).

Not all of our celebrations, however, are strictly tied to the religious calendar, as anyone who has attended the annual New Years Eve Party can attest. One of the rector's standing jokes about this popular hors

d'oeuvres party, which ends at 8 p.m. in celebration beneath a special
clock showing "midnight," is his guarantee that afterwards, party-goers
"can all be in bed, asleep by 9:00!" Another indoor revel enjoyed by many
in the parish family is the "Burns Night Dinner," an event in January
filling the church with "Kirkin o' the Tartans" bagpipes, followed by wee
drams of scotch, haggis, and other Scottish "delicacies" consumed in
Brackenridge Hall to the recitation of Robbie Burns' poetry.

In May, once the rector has consulted the Minnesota Weather
Calendar so as to avoid the last frost of the "W" season, our gatherings
move outdoors. We assemble one Sunday morning in non-church clothes
to plant the Oasis Garden that surrounds our spiritual oasis. Thousands
of colorful impatiens and other annual flowers fill that now-public space
to please us and our friends who visit. Then, in July, we celebrate the
growth of those miracles with a parish "Oasis Party" in the courtyard.
That pleasant courtyard is also the scene of post-church coffee hours in
the summer months as well as worship services on two summer Sundays.
These events afford an opportunity for all to enjoy the world's only
English-style garden with a dramatic Mayo Clinic backdrop.

Father Nick — to whom we owe the "Oasis" theme and concept
— has also instituted the October tradition of Calvary's "Stone Throw" in
which parishioners compete at tossing a large, heavy stone for distance
out in the courtyard. Father Nick claims the stone was originally thrown
back in 1860 by Bishop Whipple and Rochester's first mayor to determine
who would own the land on which Calvary stands. Apparently, the church
prevailed. These and other celebrations too numerous to cite have helped to
characterize a vibrant parish life at Calvary over these many years.

INDEX

Page numbers in boldface refer to photographs.

Ackerman, Alan, 67–68, 72
Ackerman, Archie, 169
Ackerman, Peg, **154**
Ackerman, Shirley, 67
administration, lay leadership of, 64
adult education, 78, 85–89
Agape Meal, 192
Alden, Betty, 132
Alexander, J. B., 21
Alleluia banners, 80
Allen, Anne, 9, 17
Allen, George, 25
Allen, Samuel, **164**
altar, color plates 23–24
        hangings, 99
        renovation (1978), 42
        reredos above, 40, color plate 11
        stained-glass windows above, 36, 46, 67, color plate 1
Altar Guild, 91–101
ambulatory, 41, 42, 47–48
Ameigh, John D., 26
Arrindell, Sally, **138**
aumbry, 98
Avery, Rev. R. N., 57

Baihly Farm, 167, 171
baptismal font, 33, 55, 68, 94, color plate 13
baptisms, color plate 16
Bartell, Ted, 3
Baruch, Bernard, 154
Bastian, Huber, 47
bats, 94
bazaar, 124
Behe, Azemera, 134
bells, hand-, 115

bells and bell tower, 24, 37, 38, 40, **50**
Beltz, Leah, **82**
Benedictine Way, 87
Berkman, Dulcie, 189–190
Berkman, Frances, 153, **154**, 180
Bible, lectern, 24
Bird, Ann, 47
Bird, William, 47
Blackmum, Harry, 170
Blakely, Amelia, 47
Blakely, Amerst, 47
Blakely, David, 18, 20, 21, 26
Blakely, Q. B., 47
Blakely, S. See Serena Blakely.
Blakely, Serena, 47, 117
Book of Common Prayer, 10, 94, 108
Boynton, Gertrude, 187–188
boys' choir, 104, 105–108
Boy Scouts, 70, 120
Brackenridge, Margaret, 23, 47, 68, 117, **119**, 184
Brackenridge, Walter, 23
Brackenridge Hall, 34, 37, 39, 40, 73, 74, 121
Brataas, M. G., 175
bread, Eucharistic, 96, 100
Breck, Rev. James Lloyd, 12–13, 15
Broadway, 18
Brown, Adelaide, 47
Brown, Rev. G. L. "Father Brown," 60, 141–144, **145**
Brown, William, 47
building projects
        columbarium, 42
        Crawford's contributions, 36–38
        expansion (1868), 31–33
        original chapel, 20–21, 29–32
        Spiritual Oasis Project, 42–44
        after tornado of 1883, 34–35
        after World War II, 38–42

Burns Night Dinner, 193
Bush, Barbara, 162
Bussey, Meg, 62, 79
Bussey, Rev. Lawrence, 62, 79, 155
Butler, Mrs. H. C., 68
Butler, Henry Curtis, 47
Butler, Louise, 70
Butler, Martha, 47

Calvary Episcopal Church, founding of, 17–27. See also specific entries
Calvary Episcopal Churchwomen (CEC), 123–125
Campbell, R. E., 169, 175
camps
        boys' choir, 102, 106
        Cass Lake, 72, 82, 137
Carlson, Jim, 182
Carryer, Peter, 76
Cass Lake camp, 72, 82, 137
CEC (Calvary Episcopal Churchwomen), 123–125
chalice, 98, color plate 17
chandeliers, 34
chapel, original, 20–21, 29–32
chaplains, 141–150
Chapman, Rev. Justin, 176
Charboneau, Cathy, **93**
Charboneau, Nick, photo by, color plate 18
Charboneau, William "Bill"
        Oasis Garden leadership, 3
        photos by, **7**, **90**, color plates 1, 16, 19, 21, 26
charitable works. See outreach
children's choir, 110, 111–112
children's Sunday School. See Sunday School
choirs
        boys', 104, 105–108
        children's, 110, 111–112
        early years, 119–120
        Junior, 71
        Motet, 110, color plate 19
        worship service participation, 113
Christ Church, St. Paul, 13
Christenson, Gertrude, **154**
Christmas

early interior decoration, **32**, 56
early youth group party for underprivileged children, 120
first service, 22
fruitcake sales, 121, 124, 125, 153–163, 185–187, color plate 15
packages for State Hospital patients, **122**
services, 113
Sunday School pageants, 71–72, 77, 79–80
Church of England, 9
Church Women United (CWU), 131–132
Civil War, 29
Claydon, J. A., 175
clergy, chronology of, 50–64. See also specific names of clergy
Coer, Rev. Charles T., 56
coffee hour, 88–89
Cole, John C., 27
Colquhoun, Rev. J. Ross, 59
columbarium, 42
Colvin, Irene, 186
community outreach. See outreach
concerts, in Oasis Garden, 4, 137
construction projects. See building projects
Cook, Rev. Samuel, 40, 42, 45, **52**, 61–62, 77, 78, 123, **130**, 131–133
cooking, by women's groups, 120–121
core groups, 64
cornerstones, 21, 29, 45, 163
courtyard and garden, 3–5, 137, 193, color plates 26, 28
Cowles, Mrs. Torris, 104
Crawford, Harold, 36–38, 42, 44–45, 46, 48, 107, color plate 8
Crawford, May, 107, 115
Crawford Cross, 42, 123, color plate 25
Crawford Hall, 44–45, 46, 88
Crenshaw, Nell, 153, **154**
Crop Walk, 135
Cross, Robert W., 169
Crowle, Rev. Wesley E., 146–149
CWU (Church Women United), 131–132

Daehn, Jeffrey, 112, 113
Dakota, 12

Dakota War, 22
Daup, Rev. William Wesley, **52**, 59
deacons, 64–65
Design Partners of Stiehm & Durhman, ii
Devine, Evie, 124, 185
Dines, Bette, 45–46, 48, 77, color plate 9
Dines, David, 46, 48
Dines, Sarah, 46
Dingel, Nancy. See Nancy Haworth Dingel.
Dingel, Nancy Haworth, 85, **158**
Diocese of Minnesota, 14, 23, 53, 128, 148–149, 150, 173, 175
dioceses, organization of, 10–11
Dix, Rev. Morgan, 20, 29, 128
Domestic and Foreign Missionary Society, 11
Doty, Marie, 124
Doty, Rae, 154
Drop-in Center, 131–132
Duffy, Penelope S. See Penny Duffy.
Duffy, Penny, photos by, **50**, **84**, **101**, **190**, color plates 6, 11–13, 17, 20, 22, 24–25, 27
Duffy, Sally, 124
Duncanson, Helen, 186
Durhman, Amanda, photos by, color plates 2–5, 7
Durhman, Marjorie, ii

Easter services, 114
Easter story program, 72
Eaton, Burt W., 25
ecumenism, 134–135, 138, 146–147, 149, 190
educational building, 40–41, 44, 48–49, 78, color plate 27
Education for Ministry (EfM), 87–88
Edwards, Cara, photos by, **112**, color plate 15
Engelbert, Mr. and Mrs. John, 190
Engle, Vera, **154**
Enmegabowh, 13
entrances, 35, color plate 21
Epiphany, 79–80, color plate 14
episcopal, definition of, 11
Episcopal Church
    dioceses organization, 10–11
    in frontier Minnesota, 8–15
    membership, 77
    mission work, 11

Episcopal Pastoral Services, 151
Eppard, Kay, **124**
Eucharist, 94, 96, 98, 100

facilities. See building projects
Faitoute, Abbie Frances W., 23, 47, 68
Faitoute, Samuel, 23, 47
Faribault, Minn., 13, 15, 51
Father Brown, 60, 141–144, **145**
Fay, Moses W., 27
Feith Family Statuary Park, 6, 43
fellowship, 192–193. See also parties and celebrations
Fenwick, John Leopold, 106–107
Fenwick, Rev. Robert, 61, 77, 107, 169, 174, 175
festivals. See parties and celebrations
Fidler, Mary, 186
First Ward School, 20
FISH-nets (Fellowship in Shared Homes), 86
flood of 1978, 62, 132–133
flowers, 93–94, 97
Folk Choir, 110
Forum, **84**, 88–89
founders, 18, 24–27
Fowler, Rev. William Wallace, 48, **52**, 57–58, 69, 104
Frontiers of Faith, 87
fruitcake sales, 121, 124, 125, 153–163, 185–187, color plate 15
fundraising
    Altar Guild, 94
    of founders, 20
    fruitcake sales, 162–163
    for Heifer Project, 80, 136
    for organs, 23–24
    pew rentals, 32
    Spiritual Oasis Project, 44, 81, 123
    St. Luke's, 172
    women's groups, 118, 119–120, 123
    youth groups, 71, 72

Gear, Rev. Ezekiel, 12
Gebramlak, Azmeria, 133
General Convention, 10, 14
Gibilisco, Joseph A., 165, 169, 175, 188
Gilbert, Rt. Rev. Mahlon Norris, 48

Giles, Marrieta, 186
Girl Scouts, 70, 120
Girls' Friendly Society, 36, 59, 70, 93
Goette, Mary, 134
Gooding, Frances, 40, 47
Graham, Blanche, 37, 47, 83, 109, 121
Graham, Christopher "Kit," 36, 46, 47, 67, 83, 184
Graham, Edith, 184
Graham, Jane T., 36, 46
Graham, John, 47
Graham, Joseph, 36, 46
Graham, Musetta, 47
Graham, Richard, 47
Graham, William, 23, 30–31
Green, Herman C., 18, 26
Guild Hall, 34–35, 68, 118
Gull Lake, 13
Gustafson, Mary, 86, 110
Gustafson, Ray, 110

Haines, Carrie, 47
Haines, John, 184
Haiti mission trip, 126, 136–137
Hallett, Rev. Leslie, 60, 144–146, 181
Hallett, Rosa, 145
Hallett, Rev. Timothy, 141, 145–146, 179–181
handbells, 115
hangings, altar, 99
Hargesheimer, Lee, 169
Hargesheimer, Peg, 153
harpsichord, 115
Harris, David, 109, 191
Harris, Rev. Edward "Jed," 65, **136**
Hassell, Mary, 132
Hawthorne, Dottie, 85, 86, 127
Hawthorne, Frank, 86, **126**, 127, **136**, 192–193
Head, George, 17–18, 21, 25, 117
Head, Henrietta, 25, 117
Heifer Project International, 80–81, 136
Heins, Cindy, **158**, 159
Heins, Claire, **158**
Heins, Marvin W., 165, 175, 188
Helen B. Judd Group, 76
Henderson, Edward, 144, **145**, 172

Henderson, Mabel, 153
High Church Episcopalians, 14–15
Hilker, Betsy, 154, 186
Hmong families, 133–134
Hole-in-the-Day, 13
Holtegaard, Betty, 186
Holy Week, 114
Horton, Hiram T., 21
hospital chaplains, 141–150
Hunter, Al, 49
Hunter, Sandra, 49
Hurlbut, William D., 18, 21, 26
Hurricane Katrina, 82, 137
Husband, Richard L., 48
hymns and hymnals, 103, 108, 109, 111

IBM, 166
ice cream parlor, 118
ice-cream socials, 72
inter-faith efforts and programs, 134–135, 138, 146–147, 149, 190
Inwards family, 49

Jarman, Ian, photo by, color plate 14
Johnson, E. W., 169, 175
Johnson, Wes, 173
Johnstone, Rev. William J., 31, 32, 53–54, 68
Journeys in Faith, 87
Judd, Cornelius M., 46, 83, 104
Judd, Edward J., 46
Judd, Emma F., 46
Judd, Emma J., 83, 104
Judd, E. Starr, 83, 104
Junior Aid, 123
Junior Altar Guild, 94
Junior Choir, 71

Karcher, Rev. John Keble, 56
Karsell, Kay, 78, 136, **158**
Karsell, Phil, 87, **126**, 136, **138**
Keeler, Rt. Rev. Stephen, 77, 168
Kellogg, Frank, 25, 83
Kellogg, Rt. Rev. Hamilton, 146, **164**, 165, 171–172, 175
Kemmer, David, 187

Kemper, Rt. Rev. Jackson, **11**, 12, 13, 18–19
Kettlehut, Beanie, 124
Kilbourne, A. F., 83, 106
Kirklin, Eleanor Judd, 49, 124, 153–155, 160, 169
kitchen, 35, 153, 155–156
Kjerland Stained Glass Studio, 48, color plate 7
Klampe, E. J., 73, 175
Klampe, Mrs. Everett, 73
kneelers, 45–46, color plates 9–10
Knutson, Ginger, 186
Korstad, Jerry, **159**
Kruschke, Herman, 33
Kruse, Mrs., 154

Ladies Parish Aid Society, 68, 117–122, 129, 130
Laedtke, G. M., 175
Lamberg, Carol, 159, 182
land, 20–21
Larson, Dean, 48
Larson, Jan, 48, 117, 123, **152**, 153–163, 185–187
Lay Eucharistic Visitors, 151
lay leadership, 64
Leech Lake, 13
Lent, 113–114
Lenten Bread recipe, 100
Lenten mite boxes, 71, 78, 129
Leonard, D. A., 175
lighting, 34
Lindsley, Charles H., 21
linens, altar, 98–99
liturgy and worship services
    changes (1970s), 108
    early years, 19
    hymns and hymnals, 103, 108, 109, 111
    Rite I and II use, 113
    separate children's services, 69, 189
    special services, 113–114
    Thanksgiving services, 104, 175
    youth-led, 72–73, 82
Low Church Episcopalians, 14–15
Lowry, Elizabeth G., 108–109
Lowry, Mark, 110
Lucey, Harry R., 105–106
lych-gate, **37**, 38, 41, 60, color plate 20

Malloy, Nancy, 79–80, 136
Mangan, Martha, 85, 86
Manning, Preston, 76
Markham, Grace, 154
Martens, T. G., 175
Martin, Hazel, 107–108, 114–115, 181
Mathieson, Ines, **158**
Mayo, Charles H. "Charlie," 34, 43, 130
Mayo, Charles W. "Chuck," 40, 146
Mayo, Edith Graham, 36, 46, 47, 67
Mayo, Louise, 23, 104
Mayo, William James "Will," 34, 43, 130, 188
Mayo, William Worrall, 22, 34, 43, 130
Mayo Clinic and Foundation
    Calvary's ministry to patients and employees of,
        131–132, 137–138
    Feith Family Statuary Park property, 5–6, 43
    growth of, 42–43, 166
    hospital chaplains, 141–151
    offer to purchase Calvary (1950s), 39, 166–170
McCutcheon, Thomas, 33
McDermott, Maude, 184
McDermott, Minnie, 184
McGinnis, Rev. O. Wendell, 38, 41, 48, **52**, 60–61, 76, 123,
    164, 168, 169, 173–174
McGuire, Marlene, 131–132
McNairy, Rt. Rev. Philip, 146, 188
McRoberts, J. William, 76
Medical Museum, 179
Melcher, George, 105
melodeon, 23–24, 103
membership numbers, 23, 39, 61, 62
Menefee, Rev. Guy Clifton, 38, **52**, 58–59, 71, 73–76, 142,
    145
Menefee Hall, 46
Methodist Hospital, 146–150
Mezacapa, Edna, 63
Mezacapa, Rev. Nicklas A., **4**, 7, 44, 62–64, 79, 135,
    137–138, 151, 193
missionaries, 11–12, 13
mission congregations, 173, 176. See also St. Luke's
mission statement, 6–7
mission trips, 126, 136–137
mission work. See outreach

Moore, John Arman, 18, 25
Morton Hall, 19, 20
Motet Choir, 110, color plate 19
Mother Alfred, 34, 43
Mues, Rev. Steve, 151
music
    Calvary's commitment and approach to, 103, 110–111
    instruments, 110, 114–115
    women's groups' support of, 119–120
    See also choirs; liturgy and worship services; organs

naming, of Calvary Episcopal Church, 20
Native Americans, 12–13, 22, 82
nave, color plate 23
    original, 31, 35
    redecoration (1960s), 40
    stained-glass windows, 47, 48, color plates 2–4, 23
Near, Gerald, 108–109
needlepoint kneeler cushions, 45–46, color plate 9–10
New, Ethel, 153
New Years Eve Party, 192–193
Noehren, Robert, 109

Oakwood Cemetery, 53, 58, 60, 61
Oasis courtyard and garden, 3–5, 137, 193, color plates 26, 28
Oasis Party, 193
office hours, 2, 145
Ojibwe, 12–13, 82
Olmsted County Democrat, 104
Orff instruments, 110, 115
organs
    Mason & Hamlin, 103–104
    melodeon, 23–24, 103
    Noehren-Harris (current), 41, 108–109, 112–113, 190–192
    Plummer gift, 188
    W.W. Kimball, 35, 104–105, 107
outreach
    Altar Guild funds, 94
    Christmas party for underprivileged youth, 120
    committees, 135
    Crop Walk, 135
    to downtown community, 137–138
    Drop-in Center, 131–132
    early years, 11, 128–130
    Heifer Project International, 80–81, 136
    mission trips, 126, 136–137
    refugee resettlement, 133–134
Oxford Movement, 92

Padzieski, Rev. Virginia "Ginny," 65, 81, 123
pancake supper, 78
parking, 6
parties and celebrations
    Christmas party for underprivileged youth, 120
    early years, 184–185
    New Years Eve, 192–193
    "Oasis," 193
    St. Nicholas, 81
    Stone Throw, 193
    U.S.O., 121, 130
Paulson, Rev. Peter, 61, 77, 164
Peck, Marilyn, **93**
Peck, Rev. James, 42
Pemberton, Anna, 72, 153, 154, 180–181
Pemberton, John de J., 144, **145**
pew rentals, 32
pews, 21, 35
Pfab, Rev. Martin W., 150
pianos, 114–115
Pie Patrol, 182
Pill Hill, 36–37
Pittsburgh Glass, 36, 47–48
Plummer, Daisy, 180, 188
Provoost, Rt. Rev. Samuel, 10
pulpits, 33, 99

rectories, 34, 36, 38, 62, 63, 78, 118
Red Oaks, 26
Reed, Fred, 48
refugee resettlement, 133–134
reredos, 40, color plate 11

Reynolds, Frances, 61, 76, 77
Reynolds, Larry, 109–110
Richer, Claire, **82**
Rite I and II, 113
Rochester, Minn.
    Calvary as spiritual oasis in downtown, 1–7
    early photograph, **16**
    founding of, 17–18
Rochester *City Post*, 17, 19, 22, 26
Rochester *Post-Bulletin*, 171, 172–173
Rochester Stained Glass Window Co., 47, 48
Roenigk, Julie, 85, 86
    photos by, 152, 158, 159
Roesler, Robert, 172
Rosson, Ashleigh, **136**
Rowley, Walter, 184
rummage sales, 119, 123, 124

Sachs, Arthur, 48
Sanders, Curt, photo by, **63**
Sanford, Rev. David, 19, 51, 54
Sargent's Nursery, 3
Schlitgus, Ernest, 102, 105
Schori, Most Rev. Katharine Jefferts, 125
Schuster, Frederick William, 42
Scott, Ven. Canon Benjamin Ives, 29, 47, 51, 133
Scott, Jennie Alice, 47
Scott, Sally. See Sarah Scott.
Scott, Sarah, 47, 133
Seabrease, Rev. Alexander W., 55
Seabury, Rt. Rev. Samuel, 10
Seabury Divinity School, 13, 15, 33
Seaman, Mr., 181
Seaman house, 36
Senjem, Barbara, **158**
Sermon on the Mount window, 41, 47, 48, color
    plate 6
sewing projects, 120
Sewing Society, 22, 23–24, 69, 103–104, 116, 117,
    129
Shattuck School, 15
Shedd, William, 175
Shick, Ginny, **154**
Sidewalk Café, 138

Sinclair, Margaret, **124**
Sisters of St. Francis, 34
Skattum, Paul, **138**
small groups, 86–88
social action. See outreach
Sparks, Rev. Douglas, 151, 176
Spiritual Oasis Project, 42–44, 81, 123
Spittel, Beverly, 48
Spittel, John, 48
Spor, Rev. Alpheus, 54–55
square dancing, 73
stained-glass windows, color plates 1–7
    above altar, 36, 46, 67, color plate 1
    donations, 36, 46–49
    original, 32
    Sermon on the Mount, 41, 47, 48, color plate 6
    St. Cecilia, 46, 104
St. Cecilia Choir School, 110
St. Cecilia window, 46, 104
Steinway pianos, 114–115
Stilwell, G. G., 169, 170
St. John the Evangelist Roman Catholic Church, 5–6
St. Luke's
    founding of, 39, 77, 165–176
    joint programs with Calvary, 78, 175–176
    organ, 188
    Rev. Fenwick, 61, 77
    Rev. Sparks, 151
St. Margaret's Altar Guild, 91–101
St. Margaret's Guild, 70, 95, 119, 121, 122
St. Mary's Hall, 15
St. Marys Hospital, 34, 130, 146–150
Stone Throw, 193
stove, old black gas, 155–156
St. Paul, Minn., 12–13
St. Peter's, Kasson, 176
Sudanese refugees, 133
Sunday School
    Christmas pageants, 71–72, 77, 79–80
    current curriculum and focus, 81–82
    Dulcie Berkman's recollections, 189–190
    early teachers, 83
    educational building, 40–41, **44**, 48–49, 78, color
        plate 27

enrollment numbers, 61, 76, 77, 78
  first, 68–69
  Heifer Project International, 80–81, 136
  overcrowding after WWII, 73–76
  Pupil's Note Book, 187–188
  students and teachers (2003), color plate 18
Tashjian, Alice, 175
Taylor, Rev. A. R., 57
TEC (Teens Encounter Christ), 78–79
Thanksgiving services, 104, 175
Tiffany glass, 36, 46, 47, 67, color plates 1–4
Toman, Barbara, 67, 85, 117, 183–185, 186, 187–188
Tong Pao family, **132**
tornado of 1883, 34, 129–130
Tow, Mabel, 73
Trinity Church, New York City, 20, 29
Trinity Church, St. Charles, 33
Trost, Lillian, 107
Twentyman, Margaret "Peg," 132, 133–134, 189
Twentyman, Rev. Donald, 65

Ungemach, Hazel, 184
Union National Bank building, 18
United Thank Offering (U.T.O.) drives, 130
U.S.O. parties, 121, 130

Vacation Bible School, 77, 78
Van Dooser, J. F., 18, 25
Van Dooser, Sarah, 25
VanZant, Claire, 186
Vaughn, John, 76
Vaughn, Virginia, **154**, **159**, 185–186
vessels, Eucharist, 98
vestibule, 35, 37, 38, 48
vestments, 99, 119
Virginia Hotel, 179
Visitor, 71, 72, 73, 74, 76, 130, 180
Voskuil, John, 169, 175

Waldron, Mrs. George Washington, 47
Waldron, Mr. and Mrs. Robert, 184
Waldron, Rodney, 69, 183, 184, 185
Walker, Rev. Jason F., **52** , 55–56
watercolors, 45, 46, color plate 8

Waters, George F., 48, 169
Waters, Glen Meyers, 48
Watson, Frank, 42
Weber, Mrs., 186
Wednesday Morning small group, 86
Weston, Rt. Rev. Frank, 127
Whalen, Miss, 104
Whipple, Rt. Rev. Henry Benjamin, 14–15, 19, 20, 23, 29, 48, 51, 53, 128, 193
White, Loomis, 22
White, Rt. Rev. William, 10
Williams, Brian, 103, **112**, 190–192, color plate 19
Williams, Mark, photo by, **82**
Willson, Annie, 23, 26
Willson, Bunn T., 26
Willson, Charles, 18, **19**, 20, 23, 25–26, 83
Willson, Emily, 83
Willson, Laura, 83
windows. See stained-glass windows
Winters, Sarah, 86
Woman's Auxiliary, 119, 121, 122–123
women and women's groups
  Calvary Episcopal Churchwomen, 123–125
  deacons, 65
  fruitcake project, 121, 124, 125, 153–163, 185–187
  Ladies Parish Aid Society, 68, 117–122, 119, 129, 130
  names of groups for, 118–119
  Sewing Society, 22, 23–24, 69, 103–104, 116, 117, 129
  St. Margaret's Guild, 70, 95, 119, 121, 122
  Woman's Auxiliary, 119, 121, 122–123
Wood, Harry, 48
Woodward, Charlotte, 117
Woodward, Rev. Charles, 19–25, 29, 30–31, 47, 52–53, 103, 129
woodwork, 33
World War II, 121
worship services. See liturgy and worship services
Wurtele, Rev. Arthur H., 36, 38, **52**, 58–59, 69, 92, 105, **107**

Younger, Garland C., 169
Younglove, Cornelius S., 27

Young People's Fellowship (Y.P.F.), 72–73, 120, 190
Young Peoples Guild, 183–185
youth and youth groups
    in 1960s, 76
    current service focus, 82
    first/early, 69–70, 130, 183–185
    Girls' Friendly Society, 36, 59, 70, 93
    mission trips, 137
    Scouts, 70, 120
    TEC (Teens Encounter Christ), 78–79
    worship services led by, 72–73, 82
    Young People's Fellowship (Y.P.F.), 72–73, 120,
      190
    See also Sunday School

Zumbro River, 17–18, 132